Edward Albee was born March 12, 1928. Thirty years later—having spent much of the intervening time composing poetry and beginning novels which, in his present opinion, were not much good—he turned his attention to the theatre, and began writing plays.

He has written five: THE ZOO STORY (1958); THE DEATH OF BESSIE SMITH (1959); THE SANDBOX (1959); THE AMERICAN DREAM (1960); and WHO'S AFRAID OF VIRGINIA WOOLF? (1961-62).

The first four were performed off-Broadway to a steadily mounting chorus of enthusiasm and acclaim. WHO'S AFRAID OF VIRGINIA WOOLF? appeared on Broadway with fantastic success both critically and at the box office. It received the New York Drama Critics Circle and the Tony Awards as the Best Play of the 1962-63 season.

Edward Albee's plays have also been performed in Berlin, London, Tokyo, Buenos Aires, Istanbul, Stockholm and Dublin. He lives in New York City.

Who's Afraid of Virginia Woolf? was originally published by Atheneum Publishers.

PETER W. DEVINE

Other books by Edward Albee

A Delicate Balance
Tiny Alice

Published by Pocket Books

Are there paperbound books you want but cannot find in your retail stores?

You can get any title in print in:
Pocket Book editions • Pocket *Cardinal* editions • Permabook editions or Washington Square Press editions. Simply send retail price, local sales tax, if any, plus 15¢ to cover mailing and handling costs for each book wanted to:

MAIL SERVICE DEPARTMENT
   POCKET BOOKS • A Division of Simon & Schuster, Inc.
   1 West 39th Street   •   New York, New York 10018
   Please send check or money order. We cannot be responsible for cash.
   Catalogue sent free on request.

Titles in these series are also available at discounts in quantity lots for industrial or sales-promotional use. For details write our Special Projects Agency: The Benjamin Company, Inc., 485 Madison Avenue, New York, N.Y. 10022.

Who's Afraid of Virginia Woolf?

a play by
Edward Albee

A POCKET CARDINAL EDITION
PUBLISHED BY POCKET BOOKS · NEW YORK

WHO'S AFRAID OF VIRGINIA WOOLF?

Atheneum edition published December, 1962

A Pocket *Cardinal* edition

1st printing.......November, 1963
14th printing.........March, 1969

This Pocket *Cardinal*® edition includes every word contained in the original, higher-priced edition. It is printed from brand-new plates made from completely reset, clear, easy-to-read type.

Pocket *Cardinal* editions are published by Pocket Books, a division of Simon & Schuster, Inc., 630 Fifth Avenue, New York, N.Y. 10020. Trademarks registered in the United States and other countries.

L

FIRST PERFORMANCE

October 13, 1962, New York City, Billy Rose Theatre

UTA HAGEN *as* MARTHA

ARTHUR HILL *as* GEORGE

GEORGE GRIZZARD *as* NICK

MELINDA DILLON *as* HONEY

Directed by ALAN SCHNEIDER

THE PLAYERS

MARTHA
A large, boisterous woman, 52, looking somewhat younger.
Ample, but not fleshy.

GEORGE
Her husband, 46. Thin; hair going gray.

HONEY
26, a petite blond girl, rather plain.

NICK
30, her husband. Blond, well put-together, good looking.

THE SCENE

The living room of a house on the campus of a small New
England college.

ACT ONE

FUN AND GAMES

(Set in darkness. Crash against front door. MARTHA'S *laughter heard. Front door opens, lights are switched on.* MARTHA *enters, followed by* GEORGE*)*

MARTHA

Jesus. . . .

GEORGE

. . . Shhhhhh. . . .

MARTHA

. . . H. Christ. . . .

GEORGE

For God's sake, Martha, it's two o'clock in the. . . .

MARTHA

Oh, George!

GEORGE

Well, I'm *sorry*, but. . . .

MARTHA

What a cluck! What a cluck you are.

GEORGE

It's late, you know? Late.

MARTHA

(Looks about the room. Imitates Bette Davis)
What a dump. Hey, what's that from? "What a dump!"

GEORGE

How would I know what. . . .

MARTHA

Aw, come on! What's it from? *You* know. . . .

GEORGE

. . . Martha. . . .

MARTHA

WHAT'S IT FROM, FOR CHRIST'S SAKE?

GEORGE *(Wearily)*

What's what from?

MARTHA

I just told you; I just did it. "What a dump!" Hunh?
What's that from?

GEORGE

I haven't the faintest idea what. . . .

MARTHA

Dumbbell! It's from some goddamn Bette Davis picture
. . . some goddamn Warner Brothers epic. . . .

GEORGE

I can't remember all the pictures that. . . .

MARTHA

Nobody's asking you to remember every single goddamn
Warner Brothers epic . . . just one! One single little epic!
Bette Davis gets peritonitis in the end . . . she's got this
big black fright wig she wears all through the picture and
she gets peritonitis, and she's married to Joseph Cotten
or something. . . .

GEORGE

. . . Some*body*. . . .

MARTHA

. . . some*body* . . . and she wants to go to Chicago all the time, 'cause she's in love with that actor with the scar. . . . But she gets sick, and she sits down in front of her dressing table. . . .

GEORGE

What actor? What scar?

MARTHA

I can't remember his name, for God's sake. What's the name of the *picture?* I want to know what the name of the *picture* is. She sits down in front of her dressing table . . . and she's got this peritonitis . . . and she tries to put her lipstick on, but she can't . . . and she gets it all over her face . . . but she decides to go to Chicago anyway, and. . . .

GEORGE

Chicago! It's called *Chicago*.

MARTHA

Hunh? What . . . what is?

GEORGE

The picture . . . it's called *Chicago*. . . .

MARTHA

Good grief! Don't you know *anything? Chicago* was a 'thirties musical, starring little Miss Alice *Faye*. Don't you know *anything?*

GEORGE

Well, that was probably before my *time*, but. . . .

MARTHA

Can it! Just cut that out! This picture . . . Bette Davis
comes home from a hard day at the grocery store. . . .

GEORGE

She works in a grocery store?

MARTHA

She's a housewife; she buys things . . . and she comes
home with the groceries, and she walks into the modest
living room of the modest cottage modest Joseph Cotten
has set her up in. . . .

GEORGE

Are they married?

MARTHA *(Impatiently)*

Yes. They're married. To each other. Cluck! And she
comes in, and she looks around, and she puts her groceries
down, and she says, "What a dump!"

GEORGE

(Pause) Oh.

MARTHA

(Pause) She's discontent.

GEORGE

(Pause) Oh.

MARTHA

(Pause) Well, what's the name of the picture?

GEORGE

I really don't know, Martha. . . .

MARTHA

Well, think!

GEORGE

I'm tired, dear . . . it's late . . . and besides. . . .

MARTHA

I don't know what you're so tired about . . . you haven't *done* anything all day; you didn't have any classes, or anything. . . .

GEORGE

Well, I'm tired. . . . If your father didn't set up these god-damn Saturday night orgies all the time. . . .

MARTHA

Well, that's too bad about you, George. . . .

GEORGE *(Grumbling)*

Well, that's how it is, anyway.

MARTHA

You didn't *do* anything; you never *do* anything; you never *mix.* You just sit around and *talk.*

GEORGE

What do you want me to do? Do you want me to act like you? Do you want me to go around all night *braying* at everybody, the way you do?

MARTHA *(Braying)*

I DON'T BRAY!

GEORGE *(Softly)*

All right . . . you don't bray.

MARTHA *(Hurt)*

I do not *bray.*

GEORGE

All right. I said you didn't bray.

MARTHA *(Pouting)*

Make me a drink.

GEORGE

What?

MARTHA *(Still softly)*

I said, make me a drink.

GEORGE
(Moving to the portable bar)

Well, I don't suppose a nightcap'd kill either one of
us. . . .

MARTHA

A nightcap! Are you kidding? We've got guests.

GEORGE *(Disbelieving)*

We've got what?

MARTHA

Guests. GUESTS.

GEORGE

GUESTS!

MARTHA

Yes . . . guests . . . people. . . . We've got guests coming
over.

GEORGE

When?

MARTHA

NOW!

GEORGE

Good Lord, Martha . . . do you know what time it. . . .
Who's coming over?

MARTHA

What's-their-name.

GEORGE

Who?

MARTHA

WHAT'S-THEIR-NAME!

GEORGE

Who what's-their-name?

MARTHA

I don't know what their name is, George. . . . You met them tonight . . . they're new . . . he's in the math department, or something. . . .

GEORGE

Who . . . who are these people?

MARTHA

You met them tonight, George.

GEORGE

I don't remember meeting anyone tonight. . . .

MARTHA

Well you did . . . Will you give me my drink, please. . . . He's in the math department . . . about thirty, blond, and. . . .

GEORGE

. . . and good-looking. . . .

MARTHA

Yes . . . and good-looking. . . .

GEORGE

It figures.

MARTHA

. . . and his wife's a mousey little type, without any hips,
or anything.

GEORGE (*Vaguely*)

Oh.

MARTHA

You remember them now?

GEORGE

Yes, I guess so, Martha. . . . But why in God's name are
they coming over here now?

MARTHA
(*In a so-there voice*)

Because Daddy said we should be nice to them, that's
why.

GEORGE (*Defeated*)

Oh, Lord.

MARTHA

May I have my drink, please? Daddy said we should be
nice to them. Thank you.

GEORGE

But why now? It's after two o'clock in the morning,
and. . . .

MARTHA

Because Daddy said we should be nice to them!

GEORGE

Yes. But I'm sure your father didn't mean we were supposed to stay up all *night* with these people. I mean, we

could have them over some Sunday or something. . . .

MARTHA
Well, never mind. . . . Besides, it *is* Sunday. Very early Sunday.

GEORGE
I mean . . . it's ridiculous. . . .

MARTHA
Well, it's *done!*

GEORGE
(Resigned and exasperated)
All right. Well . . . where are they? If we've got guests, where are they?

MARTHA
They'll be here soon.

GEORGE
What did they do . . . go home and get some sleep first, or something?

MARTHA
They'll *be* here!

GEORGE
I wish you'd *tell* me about something sometime. . . . I wish you'd stop *springing* things on me all the time.

MARTHA
I don't *spring* things on you all the time.

GEORGE
Yes, you do . . . you really do . . . you're always *springing* things on me.

MARTHA *(Friendly-patronizing)*

Oh, George!

GEORGE

Always.

MARTHA

Poor Georgie-Porgie, put-upon pie *(As he sulks)*
Awwwwww . . . what are you doing? Are you sulking?
Hunh? Let me see . . . are you sulking? Is that what
you're doing?

GEORGE *(Very quietly)*

Never mind, Martha. . . .

MARTHA

Awwwwwwwwww!

GEORGE

Just don't bother yourself. . . .

MARTHA

Awwwwwwwwww! *(No reaction)* Hey! *(No reaction)*
HEY!

(GEORGE looks at her, put-upon)

Hey. *(She sings)* Who's afraid of Virginia Woolf,
                                    Virginia Woolf,
                                    Virginia Woolf. . . .

Ha, ha, ha, HA! *(No reaction)* What's the matter . . .
didn't you think that was funny? Hunh? *(Defiantly)* I
thought it was a scream . . . a real scream. You didn't like
it, hunh?

GEORGE

It was all right, Martha. . . .

MARTHA

You laughed your head off when you heard it at the party.

GEORGE

I smiled. I didn't laugh my head off . . . I smiled, you
know? . . . it was all right.

MARTHA
(Gazing into her drink)
You laughed your goddamn head off.

GEORGE

It was all right. . . .

MARTHA *(Ugly)*

It was a scream!

GEORGE *(Patiently)*

It was very funny; yes.

MARTHA
(After a moment's consideration)
You make me puke!

GEORGE

What?

MARTHA

Uh . . . you make me puke!

GEORGE
(Thinks about it . . . then . . .)
That wasn't a very nice thing to say, Martha.

MARTHA

That wasn't *what?*

GEORGE

. . . a very nice thing to say.

MARTHA

I like your anger. I think that's what I like about you most

. . . your anger. You're such a . . . such a simp! You don't
even have the . . . the what? . . . .

GEORGE

. . . guts? . . . .

MARTHA

PHRASEMAKER! *(Pause . . . then they both laugh)* Hey, put
some more ice in my drink, will you? You never put any
ice in my drink. Why is that, hunh?

GEORGE *(Takes her drink)*

I always put ice in your drink. You eat it, that's all. It's
that habit you have . . . chewing your ice cubes . . . like
a cocker spaniel. You'll crack your big teeth.

MARTHA

THEY'RE MY BIG TEETH!

GEORGE

Some of them . . . some of them.

MARTHA

I've got more teeth than you've got.

GEORGE

Two more.

MARTHA

Well, two more's a lot more.

GEORGE

I suppose it is. I suppose it's pretty remarkable . . . considering how old you are.

MARTHA

YOU CUT THAT OUT! *(Pause)* You're not so young yourself.

GEORGE
(With boyish pleasure . . . a chant)
I'm six years younger than you are. . . . I always have
been and I always will be.

MARTHA *(Glumly)*
Well . . . you're going bald.

GEORGE
So are you. *(Pause . . . they both laugh)* Hello, honey.

MARTHA
Hello. C'mon over here and give your Mommy a big
sloppy kiss.

GEORGE
. . . oh, now. . . .

MARTHA
I WANT A BIG SLOPPY KISS!

GEORGE *(Preoccupied)*
I don't *want* to kiss you, Martha. Where *are* these people?
Where are these *people* you invited over?

MARTHA
They stayed on to talk to Daddy. . . . They'll be here. . . .
Why don't you want to kiss me?

GEORGE
(Too matter-of-fact)
Well, dear, if I kissed you I'd get all excited . . . I'd get beside myself, and I'd take you, by force, right here on the
living room rug, and then our little guests would walk in,
and . . . well, just think what your father would say about
that.

MARTHA

You pig!

GEORGE *(Haughtily)*

Oink! Oink!

MARTHA

Ha, ha, ha, HA! Make me another drink . . . lover.

GEORGE *(Taking her glass)*

My God, you can swill it down, can't you?

MARTHA
(Imitating a tiny child)

I'm firsty.

GEORGE

Jesus!

MARTHA *(Swinging around)*

Look, sweetheart, I can drink you under any goddamn table you want . . . so don't worry about me!

GEORGE

Martha, I gave you the prize years ago. . . . There isn't an abomination award going that you. . . .

MARTHA

I swear . . . if you existed I'd divorce you. . . .

GEORGE

Well, just stay on your feet, that's all. . . . These people are your guests, you know, and. . . .

MARTHA

I can't even see you . . . I haven't been able to see you for years. . . .

GEORGE

. . . if you pass out, or throw up, or something. . .

MARTHA

. . . I mean, you're a blank, a cipher. . . .

GEORGE

. . . and try to keep your clothes on, too. There aren't many more sickening sights than you with a couple of drinks in you and your skirt up over your head, you know. . . .

MARTHA

. . . a zero. . . .

GEORGE

. . . your *heads,* I should say. . . .
                    (The front doorbell chimes)

MARTHA

Party! Party!

GEORGE *(Murderously)*

I'm really looking forward to this, Martha. . . .

MARTHA *(Same)*

Go answer the door.

GEORGE *(Not moving)*

You answer it.

MARTHA

Get to that door, you.
                    (He does not move)
I'll fix you, you. . . .

GEORGE *(Fake-spits)*

. . . to you. . . .

(Door chime again)

MARTHA
(Shouting . . . to the door)
C'MON IN! *(To* GEORGE, *between her teeth)* I said, get over
there!

GEORGE
(Moves a little toward the door, smiling slightly)
All right, love . . . whatever love wants. *(Stops)* Just don't
start on the bit, that's all.

MARTHA
The bit? The bit? What kind of language is that? What
are you talking about?

GEORGE
The bit. Just don't start in on the bit.

MARTHA
You imitating one of your students, for God's sake? What
are you trying to do? WHAT BIT?

GEORGE
Just don't start in on the bit about the kid, that's all.

MARTHA
What do you take me for?

GEORGE
Much too much.

MARTHA *(Really angered)*
Yeah? Well, I'll start in on the kid if I want to.

GEORGE
Just leave the kid out of this.

MARTHA *(Threatening)*

He's mine as much as he is yours. I'll talk about him if I want to.

GEORGE

I'd advise against it, Martha.

MARTHA

Well, good for you. *(Knock)* C'mon in. Get over there and open the door!

GEORGE

You've been advised.

MARTHA

Yeah . . . sure. Get over there!

GEORGE

(Moving toward the door)

All right, love . . . whatever love wants. Isn't it nice the way some people have manners, though, even in this day and age? Isn't it nice that some people won't just come breaking into other people's houses even if they *do* hear some sub-human monster yowling at 'em from inside . . . ?

MARTHA

SCREW YOU! to Nick and Honey

(Simultaneously with MARTHA'S *last remark,* GEORGE *flings open the front door.* HONEY *and* NICK *are framed in the entrance. There is a brief silence, then. . . .)*

GEORGE

(Ostensibly a pleased recognition of HONEY *and* NICK, *but really satisfaction at having* MARTHA'S *explosion overheard)*

Ahhhhhhhhh!

MARTHA
(A little too loud . . . to cover)
HI! Hi, there . . . c'mon in!

HONEY *and* NICK *(ad lib)*
Hello, here we are . . . hi . . . *etc.*

GEORGE
(Very matter-of-factly)
You must be our little guests.

MARTHA
Ha, ha, ha, HA! Just ignore old sour-puss over there.
C'mon in, kids . . . give your coats and stuff to sour-puss.

NICK *(Without expression)*
Well, now, perhaps we shouldn't have come. . . .

HONEY
Yes . . . it *is* late, and. . . .

MARTHA
Late! Are you kidding? Throw your stuff down anywhere
and c'mon in.

GEORGE
(Vaguely . . . walking away)
Anywhere . . . furniture, floor . . . doesn't make any dif-
ference around this place.

NICK *(To* HONEY*)*
I told you we shouldn't have come.

MARTHA *(Stentorian)*
I said c'mon in! Now c'mon!

HONEY
(Giggling a little as she and NICK *advance)*
Oh, dear.

GEORGE
(Imitating HONEY's *giggle)*
Hee, hee, hee, hee.

MARTHA *(Swinging on* GEORGE)
Look, muckmouth . . . you cut that out!

GEORGE
(Innocence and hurt)
Martha! *(To* HONEY *and* NICK) Martha's a devil with language; she really is.

MARTHA
Hey, *kids* . . . sit down.

HONEY *(As she sits)*
Oh, isn't this lovely!

NICK *(Perfunctorily)*
Yes indeed . . . very handsome.

MARTHA
Well, thanks.

NICK
(Indicating the abstract painting)
Who . . . who did the . . . ?

MARTHA
That? Oh, that's by. . . .

GEORGE
. . . some Greek with a mustache Martha attacked one night in. . . .

HONEY
(To save the situation)

Oh, ho, ho, ho, HO.

NICK

It's got a . . . a. . . .

GEORGE

A quiet intensity?

NICK

Well, no . . . a. . . .

GEORGE

Oh. *(Pause)* Well, then, a certain noisy relaxed quality, maybe?

NICK
(Knows what GEORGE is doing, but stays grimly, coolly polite)

No. What I meant was. . . .

GEORGE

How about . . . uh . . . a quietly noisy relaxed intensity.

HONEY

Dear! You're being joshed.

NICK *(Cold)*

I'm aware of that.
(A brief, awkward silence)

GEORGE *(Truly)*

I *am* sorry.
(NICK nods condescending forgiveness)

GEORGE

What it is, actually, is it's a pictorial representation of the order of Martha's mind.

MARTHA

Ha, ha, ha, HA! Make the kids a drink, George. What do you want, kids? What do you want to drink, hunh?

NICK

Honey? What would you like?

HONEY

I don't know, dear . . . A little brandy, maybe. "Never mix—never worry." *(She giggles)*

GEORGE

Brandy? Just brandy? Simple; simple. *(Moves to the portable bar)* What about you . . . uh. . . .

NICK

Bourbon on the rocks, if you don't mind.

GEORGE *(As he makes drinks)*

Mind? No, I don't mind. I don't think I mind. Martha? Rubbing alcohol for you?

MARTHA

Sure. "Never mix—never worry."

GEORGE

Martha's tastes in liquor have come down . . . simplified over the years . . . crystallized. Back when I was courting Martha—well, I don't know if that's exactly the right word for it—but back when I was courting Martha. . . .

MARTHA *(Cheerfully)*

Screw, sweetie!

GEORGE
(Returning with HONEY and NICK's drinks)

At any rate, back when I was courting Martha, she'd order the damnedest things! You wouldn't believe it! We'd go into a bar . . . you know, a *bar* . . . a whiskey, beer, and bourbon *bar* . . . and what she'd do would be, she'd screw up her face, think real hard, and come up with . . . brandy Alexanders, crème de cacao frappés, gimlets, flaming punch bowls . . . seven-layer liqueur things.

MARTHA

They were good . . . I liked them.

GEORGE

Real lady-like little drinkies.

MARTHA

Hey, where's my rubbing alcohol?

GEORGE
(Returning to the portable bar)
But the years have brought to Martha a sense of essentials . . . the knowledge that cream is for coffee, lime juice for pies . . . and alcohol *(Brings* MARTHA *her drink)* pure and simple . . . here you are, angel . . . for the pure and simple. *(Raises his glass)* For the mind's blind eye, the heart's ease, and the liver's craw. Down the hatch, all.

MARTHA *(To them all)*
Cheers, dears. *(They all drink)* You have a poetic nature, George . . . a Dylan Thomas-y quality that gets me right where I live.

GEORGE

Vulgar girl! With guests here!

MARTHA

Ha, ha, ha, HA! *(To* HONEY *and* NICK*)* Hey; hey!
(Sings, conducts with her drink in her hand.

HONEY *joins in toward the end)*
>   Who's afraid of Virginia Woolf,
>   Virginia Woolf,
>   Virginia Woolf,
>   Who's afraid of Virginia Woolf....
>   (MARTHA *and* HONEY *laugh;* NICK *smiles)*

HONEY

Oh, wasn't that funny? That was so funny. . . .

NICK *(Snapping to)*

Yes . . . yes, it was.

MARTHA

I thought I'd bust a gut; I really did. . . . I really thought I'd bust a gut laughing. George didn't like it. . . . George didn't think it was funny at all.

GEORGE

Lord, Martha, do we have to go through this again?

MARTHA

I'm trying to shame you into a sense of humor, angel, that's all.

GEORGE
(Over-patiently, to HONEY *and* NICK*)*

Martha didn't think I laughed loud enough. Martha thinks that unless . . . as she demurely puts it . . . that unless you "bust a gut" you aren't amused. You know? Unless you carry on like a hyena you aren't having any fun.

HONEY

Well, I certainly had fun . . . it was a *wonderful* party.

NICK
(Attempting enthusiasm)

Yes . . . it certainly was.

                    HONEY (*To* MARTHA)
And your father! Oh! He is so marvelous!

                         NICK (*As above*)
Yes . . . yes, he is.

                         HONEY
Oh, I tell you.

                    MARTHA (*Genuinely proud*)
He's quite a guy, isn't he? Quite a guy.

                    GEORGE (*At* NICK)
And you'd better believe it!

                    HONEY (*Admonishing* GEORGE)
Ohhhhhhhhh! He's a wonderful man.

                         GEORGE
I'm not trying to tear him down. He's a God, we all know
that.

                         MARTHA
You lay off my father!

                         GEORGE
Yes, love. (*To* NICK) All I mean is . . . when you've had as
many of these faculty parties as I have. . . .

                         NICK
              (*Killing the attempted rapport*)
I rather appreciated it. I mean, aside from enjoying it, I
appreciated it. You know, when you're new at a place. . . .
              (GEORGE *eyes him suspiciously*)
Meeting everyone, getting introduced around . . . getting

to know some of the men. . . . When I was teaching in
Kansas. . . .

HONEY

You won't believe it, but we had to make our way all by
ourselves . . . isn't that right, dear?

NICK

Yes, it is. . . . We. . . .

HONEY

. . . We had to make our own way. . . . I had to go up to
wives . . . in the library, or at the supermarket . . . and
say, "Hello, I'm new here . . . you must be Mrs. So-and-so,
Doctor So-and-so's wife." It really wasn't very nice at all.

MARTHA

Well, *Daddy* knows how to run things.

NICK
(Not enough enthusiasm)

He's a remarkable man.

MARTHA

You bet your sweet life.

GEORGE
(To NICK *. . . a confidence, but not whispered)*

Let me tell you a secret, baby. There are easier things in
the world, if you happen to be teaching at a university,
there are easier things than being married to the daughter
of the president of that university. There are easier things
in this world.

MARTHA
(Loud . . . to no one in particular)

It *should* be an extraordinary opportunity . . . for *some*
men it would be the chance of a lifetime!

GEORGE
(To NICK *. . . a solemn wink)*

There are, believe me, easier things in this world.

NICK

Well, I can understand how it might make for some . . .
awkwardness, perhaps . . . conceivably, but. . . .

MARTHA

Some men would give their right arm for the chance!

GEORGE *(Quietly)*

Alas, Martha, in reality it works out that the sacrifice is
usually of a somewhat more private portion of the
anatomy.

MARTHA
(A snarl of dismissal and contempt)

NYYYYAAAAHHHHH!

HONEY *(Rising quickly)*

I wonder if you could show me where the . . . *(Her voice
trails off)*

GEORGE
(To MARTHA, *indicating* HONEY*)*

Martha. . . .

NICK *(To* HONEY*)*

Are you all right?

HONEY

Of course, dear. I want to . . . put some powder on my
nose.

GEORGE
(As MARTHA *is not getting up)*

Martha, won't you show her where we keep the . . . euphemism?

MARTHA

Hm? What? Oh! Sure! *(Rises)* I'm sorry, c'mon. I want to show you the house.

HONEY

I think I'd like to. . . .

MARTHA

. . . wash up? Sure . . . c'mon with me. *(Takes* HONEY *by the arm. To the men)* You two do some men talk for a while.

HONEY *(To* NICK*)*

We'll be back, dear.

MARTHA *(To* GEORGE*)*

Honestly, George, you burn me up!

GEORGE *(Happily)*

All right.

MARTHA

You really do, George.

GEORGE

O.K. Martha . . . O.K. Just . . . trot along.

MARTHA

You really do.

GEORGE

Just don't shoot your mouth off . . . about . . . you-know-what.

MARTHA
(Surprisingly vehement)
I'll talk about any goddamn thing I want to, George!

GEORGE

O.K. O.K. Vanish.

MARTHA

Any goddamn thing I want to! *(Practically dragging*
HONEY *out with her)* C'mon. . . .

GEORGE

Vanish. *(The women have gone)* So? What'll it be?

NICK

Oh, I don't know . . . I'll stick to bourbon, I guess.

GEORGE
(Takes NICK's *glass, goes to portable bar)*
That what you were drinking over at Parnassus?

NICK

Over at . . . ?

GEORGE

Parnassus.

NICK

I don't understand. . . .

GEORGE

Skip it. *(Hands him his drink)* One bourbon.

NICK

Thanks.

GEORGE

It's just a private joke between li'l ol' Martha and me.
(They sit) So? *(Pause)* So . . . you're in the math department, eh?

NICK

No . . . uh, no.

GEORGE

Martha said you were. I think that's what she said. *(Not too friendly)* What made you decide to be a teacher?

NICK

Oh . . . well, the same things that . . . uh . . . motivated you, I imagine.

GEORGE

What were they?

NICK *(Formal)*

Pardon?

GEORGE

I said, what were they? What were the things that motivated me?

NICK *(Laughing uneasily)*

Well . . . I'm sure I don't know.

GEORGE

You just finished saying that the things that motivated you you were the same things that motivated me.

NICK *(With a little pique)*

I said I *imagined* they were.

GEORGE

Oh. *(Off-hand)* Did you? *(Pause)* Well. . . . *(Pause)* You like it here?

NICK
(Looking about the room)

Yes . . . it's . . . it's fine.

GEORGE

I mean the University.

NICK

Oh. . . . I thought you meant. . . .

GEORGE

Yes . . . I can see you did. *(Pause)* I meant the University.

NICK

Well, I . . . I like it . . . fine *(As George just stares at him)* Just fine. *(Same)* You . . . you've been here quite a long time, haven't you?

GEORGE
(Absently, as if he had not heard)
What? Oh . . . yes. Ever since I married . . . uh, What's-her-name . . . uh, Martha. Even before that. *(Pause)* For-ever. *(To himself)* Dashed hopes, and good intentions. Good, better, best, bested. *(Back to* NICK*)* How do you like that for a declension, young man? Eh?

NICK

Sir, I'm sorry if we. . . .

GEORGE
(With an edge in his voice)
You didn't answer my question.

NICK

Sir?

GEORGE

Don't you condescend to me! *(Toying with him)* I asked you how you liked that for a declension: Good; better; best; bested. Hm? Well?

NICK *(With some distaste)*

I really don't know what to say.

GEORGE
(Feigned incredulousness)
You really don't know what to *say?*

NICK *(Snapping it out)*
All right . . . what do you want me to say? Do you want
me to say it's funny, so you can contradict me and say
it's sad? or do you want me to say it's sad so you can
turn around and say no, it's funny. You can play that
damn little game any way you want to, you know!

GEORGE *(Feigned awe)*
Very good! Very good!

NICK
(Even angrier than before)
And when my wife comes back, I think we'll just. . . .

GEORGE *(Sincere)*
Now, now . . . calm down, my boy. Just . . . calm . . .
down. *(Pause)* All right? *(Pause)* You want another drink?
Here, give me your glass.

NICK
I still have one. I *do* think that when my wife comes
downstairs. . . .

GEORGE
Here . . . I'll freshen it. Give me your glass. *(Takes it)*

NICK
What I mean is . . . you two . . . you and your wife . . .
seem to be having *some* sort of a. . . .

GEORGE
Martha and I are having . . . nothing. Martha and I are
merely . . . exercising . . . that's all . . . we're merely

walking what's left of our wits. Don't pay any attention to
it.

NICK *(Undecided)*

Still. . . .

GEORGE
(An abrupt change of pace)
Well, now . . . let's sit down and talk, hunh?

NICK *(Cool again)*
It's just that I don't like to . . . become involved . . . *(An
afterthought)* uh . . . in other people's affairs.

GEORGE *(Comforting a child)*
Well, you'll get over that . . . small college and all.
Musical beds is the faculty sport around here.

NICK

Sir?

GEORGE
I said, musical beds is the faculty. . . . Never mind. I wish
you wouldn't go "Sir" like that . . . not with the question
mark at the end of it. You know? Sir? I know it's meant to
be a sign of respect for your *(Winces)* elders . . . but . . .
uh . . . the way you do it. . . . Uh . . . Sir? . . .
Madam?

NICK
(With a small, noncommittal smile)
No disrespect intended.

GEORGE
How old *are* you?

NICK

Twenty-eight.

comparing masculinity

GEORGE

I'm forty something. *(Waits for reaction . . . gets none)* Aren't you surprised? I mean . . . don't I look older? Doesn't this . . . *gray* quality suggest the fifties? Don't I sort of fade into backgrounds . . . get lost in the cigarette smoke? Hunh?

NICK
(Looking around for an ash tray)
I think you look . . . fine.

GEORGE

I've always been lean . . . I haven't put on five pounds since I was your age. I don't have a paunch, either. . . . What I've got . . . I've got this little distension just below the belt . . . but it's hard . . . It's not soft flesh. I use the handball courts. How much do *you* weigh?

NICK

I. . . .

GEORGE

Hundred and fifty-five, sixty . . . something like that? Do you play handball?

NICK

Well, yes . . . no . . . I mean, not very well.

GEORGE

Well, then . . . we shall play some time. Martha is a hundred and eight . . . years *old*. She weighs somewhat more than that. How old is *your* wife?

NICK
(A little bewildered)
She's twenty-six.

GEORGE

Martha is a remarkable woman. I would imagine she weighs around a hundred and ten.

NICK

Your . . . wife . . . weighs . . . ?

GEORGE

No, no, my boy. Yours! *Your* wife. My wife is Martha.

NICK

Yes . . . I know.

GEORGE

If you were married to Martha you would know what it means. *(Pause)* But then, if I were married to your wife I would know what that means, too . . . wouldn't I?

NICK *(After a pause)*

Yes.

GEORGE

Martha says you're in the Math Department, or something.

NICK
(As if for the hundredth time)

No . . . I'm not.

GEORGE

Martha is seldom mistaken . . . maybe you *should* be in the Math Department, or something.

NICK

I'm a biologist. I'm in the Biology Department.

GEORGE
(After a pause)

Oh. *(Then, as if remembering something)* OH!

NICK

Sir?

GEORGE

You're the one! You're the one's going to make all that trouble . . . making everyone the same, rearranging the chromozones, or whatever it is. Isn't that right?

NICK *(With that small smile)*

Not exactly: chromo*somes.*

GEORGE

I'm very mistrustful. Do you believe . . . *(Shifting in his chair)* . . . do you believe that people learn nothing from history? Not that there is nothing to learn, mind you, but that people learn nothing? I am in the History Department.

NICK

Well. . . .

GEORGE

I am a Doctor. A.B. . . . M.A. . . . PH.D. . . . ABMAPHID! Abmaphid has been variously described as a wasting disease of the frontal lobes, and as a wonder drug. It is actually both. I'm really very mistrustful. Biology, hunh?

(NICK *does not answer . . . nods . . . looks)*

I read somewhere that science fiction is really not fiction at all . . . that you people are rearranging my genes, so that everyone will be like everyone else. Now, I won't have that! It would be a . . . shame. I mean . . . look at me! Is it really such a good idea . . . if everyone was forty something and looked fifty-five? You didn't answer my question about history.

NICK

This genetic business you're talking about. . .

GEORGE

Oh, that. (*Dismisses it with a wave of his hand*) That's
very upsetting . . . very . . . disappointing. But history is
a great deal more . . . disappointing. I am in the History
Department.

NICK

Yes . . . you told me.

GEORGE

I know I told you. . . . I shall probably tell you several
more times. Martha tells me often, that I am *in* the History Department . . . as opposed to *being* the History
Department . . . in the sense of *running* the History Department. I do not run the History Department.

NICK

Well, I don't run the Biology Department.

GEORGE

You're twenty-one!

NICK

Twenty-eight.

GEORGE

Twenty-eight! Perhaps when you're forty something and
look fifty-five, you will run the History Department. . . .

NICK

. . . Biology. . . .

GEORGE

. . . the Biology Department. I *did* run the History Department, for four years, during the war, but that was because
everybody was away. Then . . . everybody came back . . .
because nobody got killed. That's New England for you.

Isn't that amazing? Not one single man in this whole place got his head shot off. That's pretty irrational. *(Broods)* Your wife *doesn't* have any hips . . . has she . . . does she?

NICK

What?

GEORGE

I don't mean to suggest that I'm hip-happy. . . . I'm not one of those thirty-six, twenty-two, seventy-eight men. Nosiree . . . not me. Everything in proportion. I was implying that your wife is . . . slim-hipped.

NICK

Yes . . . she is.

GEORGE
(Looking at the ceiling)

What are they *doing* up there? I assume that's where they are.

NICK *(False heartiness)*

You know women.

GEORGE
(Gives NICK *a long stare, of feigned incredulity
. . . then his attention moves)*

Not one son-of-a-bitch got killed. Of course, nobody bombed Washington. No . . . that's not fair. You have any kids?

NICK

Uh . . . no . . . not yet. *(Pause)* You?

GEORGE
(A kind of challenge)

That's for me to know and you to find out.

NICK

Indeed?

GEORGE

No kids, hunh?

NICK

Not yet.

GEORGE

People do . . . uh . . . have kids. That's what I meant
about history. You people are going to make them in test
tubes, aren't you? You biologists. Babies. Then the rest of
us . . . them as wants to . . . can screw to their heart's
content. What will happen to the tax deduction? Has anyone figured that out yet?
  (NICK, *who can think of nothing better to do,
  laughs mildly*)
But you *are* going to have kids . . . anyway. In spite of
history.

NICK *(Hedging)*

Yes . . . certainly. We . . . want to wait . . . a little . . .
until we're settled.

GEORGE

And this . . . *(With a handsweep taking in not only the
room, the house, but the whole countryside)* . . . this is
your heart's content—Illyria . . . Penguin Island . . .
Gomorrah. . . . You think you're going to be happy here
in New Carthage, eh?

NICK *(A little defensively)*

I hope we'll stay here.

GEORGE

And every definition has its boundaries, eh? Well, it isn't

a bad college, I guess. I mean . . . it'll do. It isn't M.I.T.
. . . it isn't U.C.L.A. . . . it isn't the Sorbonne . . . or
Moscow U. either, for that matter.

NICK

I don't mean . . . forever.

GEORGE

Well, don't you let that get bandied about. The old man
wouldn't like it. Martha's father expects loyalty and de-
votion out of his . . . staff. I was going to use another word.
Martha's father expects his . . . staff . . . to cling to the
walls of this place, like the ivy . . . to come here and grow
old . . . to fall in the line of service. One man, a professor
of Latin and Elocution, actually fell in the cafeteria line,
one lunch. He was buried, as many of us have been, and
as many more of us will be, under the shrubbery around
the chapel. It is said . . . and I have no reason to doubt it
. . . that we make excellent fertilizer. But the old man is
not going to be buried under the shrubbery . . . the old
man is not going to die. Martha's father has the staying
power of one of those Micronesian tortoises. There are
rumors . . . which you must not breathe in front of Martha,
for she foams at the mouth . . . that the old man, her
father, is over two hundred years old. There is probably
an irony involved in this, but I am not drunk enough to
figure out what it is. How many kids you going to have?

NICK

I . . . I don't know. . . . My wife is. . . .

GEORGE

Slim-hipped. *(Rises)* Have a drink.

NICK

Yes.

GEORGE

MARTHA! *(No answer)* DAMN IT! *(To* NICK) You asked me
if I knew women. . . . Well, one of the things I do *not*
know about them is what they talk about while the men
are talking. *(Vaguely)* I must find out some time.

MARTHA'S VOICE

WHADD'YA WANT?

GEORGE *(To* NICK)

Isn't that a wonderful sound? What I mean is . . . what do
you think they really *talk* about . . . or don't you care?

NICK

Themselves, I would imagine.

MARTHA'S VOICE

GEORGE?

GEORGE *(To* NICK)

Do you find women . . . puzzling?

NICK

Well . . . yes and no.

GEORGE *(With a knowing nod)*

Unh-hunh. *(Moves toward the hall, almost bumps into*
HONEY, *re-entering)* Oh! Well, here's one of you, at least.
*(*HONEY *moves toward* NICK. GEORGE *goes to the hall)*

HONEY *(To* GEORGE)

She'll be right down. *(To* NICK) You must see this house,
dear . . . this is such a wonderful old house.

NICK

Yes, I. . . .

GEORGE

MARTHA!

MARTHA'S VOICE

FOR CHRIST'S SAKE, HANG ON A MINUTE, WILL YOU?

HONEY (*To* GEORGE)

She'll be right down . . . she's changing.

GEORGE (*Incredulous*)

She's *what*? She's changing?

HONEY

Yes.

GEORGE

Her clothes?

HONEY

Her dress.

GEORGE (*Suspicious*)

Why?

HONEY
(*With a nervous little laugh*)

Why, I imagine she wants to be . . . comfortable.

GEORGE
(*With a threatening look toward the hall*)

Oh she does, does she?

HONEY

Well, heavens, I should think. . . .

GEORGE

YOU DON'T KNOW!

NICK (*As* HONEY *starts*)

You feel all right?

HONEY
*(Reassuring, but with the echo of a whine. A
long-practiced tone)*
Oh, yes, dear . . . perfectly fine.

GEORGE
(Fuming . . . to himself)
So she wants to be comfortable, does she? Well, we'll see
about that.

HONEY (*To* GEORGE, *brightly*)
I didn't know until just a minute ago that you had a *son*.

GEORGE
(Wheeling, as if struck from behind)
WHAT?

HONEY
A son! I hadn't known.

NICK
You to know and me to find out. Well, he must be quite a
big. . . .

HONEY
Twenty-one . . . twenty-one tomorrow . . . tomorrow's his
birthday.

NICK (*A victorious smile*)
Well!

GEORGE (*To* HONEY)
She told you about him?

HONEY *(Flustered)*

Well, *yes*. Well, I mean. . . .

GEORGE *(Nailing it down)*

She told you about him.

HONEY *(A nervous giggle)*

Yes.

GEORGE *(Strangely)*

You say she's changing?

HONEY

Yes. . . .

GEORGE

And she mentioned . . . ?

HONEY
(Cheerful, but a little puzzled)

. . . your son's birthday . . . yes.

GEORGE
(More or less to himself)

O.K., Martha . . . O.K.

NICK

You look pale, Honey. Do you want a . . . ?

HONEY

Yes, dear . . . a little more brandy, maybe. Just a drop.

GEORGE

O.K., Martha.

NICK

May I use the . . . uh . . . bar?

GEORGE

Hm? Oh, yes . . . yes . . . by all means. Drink away . . .
you'll need it as the years go on. *(For* MARTHA, *as if she
were in the room)* You goddamn destructive. . . .

HONEY *(To cover)*

What time is it, dear?

NICK

Two-thirty.

HONEY

Oh, it's so late . . . we *should* be getting home.

GEORGE

  *(Nastily, but he is so preoccupied he hardly
  notices his own tone)*
For what? You keeping the babysitter up, or something?

NICK

  (Almost a warning)
I told you we didn't have children.

GEORGE

Hm? *(Realizing)* Oh, I'm sorry. I wasn't even listening . . .
or thinking . . . *(With a flick of his hand)* . . . whichever
one applies.

NICK *(Softly, to* HONEY*)*

We'll go in a little while.

GEORGE *(Driving)*

Oh no, now . . . you mustn't. Martha is changing . . .
and Martha is not changing for *me*. Martha hasn't
changed for *me* in years. If Martha is changing, it means
we'll be here for . . . days. You are being accorded an
honor, and you must not forget that Martha is the

daughter of our beloved boss. She is his . . . right ball, you might say.

NICK

You might not understand this . . . but I wish you wouldn't talk that way in front of my wife.

HONEY

Oh, now. . . .

GEORGE *(Incredulous)*

Really? Well, you're quite right. . . . We'll leave that sort of talk to Martha.

MARTHA *(Entering)*

What sort of talk?
(MARTHA *has changed her clothes, and she looks, now, more comfortable and . . . and this is most important . . . most voluptuous)*

GEORGE

There you are, my pet.

NICK *(Impressed; rising)*

Well, now. . . .

GEORGE

Why, Martha . . . your Sunday chapel dress!

HONEY *(Slightly disapproving)*

Oh, that's most attractive.

MARTHA *(Showing off)*

You like it? Good! *(To* GEORGE*)* What the hell do you mean screaming up the stairs at me like that?

GEORGE

We got lonely, darling . . . we got lonely for the soft purr of your little voice.

MARTHA
(Deciding not to rise to it)
Oh. Well, then, you just trot over to the barie-poo. . . .

GEORGE
(Taking the tone from her)
. . . and make your little mommy a gweat big dwink.

MARTHA *(Giggles)*
That's right. *(To* NICK*)* Well, did you two have a nice little
talk? You men solve the problems of the world, as usual?

NICK
Well, no, we . . .

GEORGE *(Quickly)*
What we did, actually, if you really want to know, what
we did actually is try to figure out what you two were
talking about.
(HONEY *giggles,* MARTHA *laughs)*

MARTHA *(To* HONEY*)*
Aren't they something? Aren't these . . . *(Cheerfully dis-
dainful)* . . . men the absolute end? *(To* GEORGE*)* Why
didn't you sneak upstairs and listen in?

GEORGE
Oh, I wouldn't have *listened,* Martha. . . . I would have
peeked.
(HONEY *giggles,* MARTHA *laughs)*

NICK
(To GEORGE, *with false heartiness)*
It's a conspiracy.

GEORGE
And now we'll never know. Shucks!

MARTHA
(To NICK, *as* HONEY *beams)*

Hey, you must be quite a boy, getting your Masters when you were . . . what? . . . twelve? You hear that, George?

NICK

Twelve-and-a-half, actually. No, nineteen really. *(To* HONEY*)* Honey, you needn't have mentioned that. It. . . .

HONEY

Ohhhh . . . I'm *proud* of you. . . .

GEORGE *(Seriously, if sadly)*

That's very . . . impressive.

MARTHA *(Aggressively)*

You're damned right!

GEORGE *(Between his teeth)*

I said I was impressed, Martha. I'm beside myself with jealousy. What do you want me to do, throw up? *(To* NICK*)* That really is very impressive. *(To* HONEY*)* You should be right proud.

HONEY *(Coy)*

Oh, he's a pretty nice fella.

GEORGE *(To* NICK*)*

I wouldn't be surprised if you *did* take over the History Department one of these days.

NICK

The Biology Department.

GEORGE

The *Biology* Department . . . of course. I seem preoccupied with history. Oh! What a remark. *(He strikes a pose, his hand over his heart, his head raised, his voice stentorian)* "I am preoccupied with history."

MARTHA
(As HONEY *and* NICK *chuckle)*
Ha, ha, ha, HA!

GEORGE *(With some disgust)*
I think I'll make *myself* a drink.

MARTHA
George is not preoccupied with *history*. . . . George is preoccupied with the *History Department*. George is preoccupied with the History Department because. . . .

GEORGE
. . . because he is *not* the History Department, but is only *in* the History Department. We know, Martha . . . we went all through it while you were upstairs . . . getting up. There's no need to go through it again.

MARTHA
That's right, baby . . . keep it clean. *(To the others)* George is bogged down in the History Department. He's an old bog in the History Department, that's what George is. A bog. . . . A fen. . . . A G.D. swamp. Ha, ha, ha HA! A SWAMP! Hey, swamp! Hey SWAMPY!

GEORGE
(With a great effort controls himself . . . then, as if she had said nothing more than "George, dear". . . .)
Yes, Martha? Can I get you something?

MARTHA *(Amused at his game)*
Well . . . uh . . . sure, you can light my cigarette, if you're of a mind to.

GEORGE
(Considers, then moves off)

No . . . there are limits. I mean, man can put up with only so much without he descends a rung or two on the old evolutionary ladder . . . *(Now a quick aside to* NICK*)* . . . which is up your line . . . *(Then back to* MARTHA*)* . . . sinks, Martha, and it's a funny ladder . . . you can't reverse yourself . . . start back up once you're descending.

*(*MARTHA *blows him an arrogant kiss)*

Now . . . I'll hold your hand when it's dark and you're afraid of the bogey man, and I'll tote your gin bottles out after midnight, so no one'll see . . . but I will not light your cigarette. And that, as they say, is that.

(Brief silence)

MARTHA *(Under her breath)*

Jesus! *(Then, immediately, to* NICK*)* Hey, you played football, hunh?

HONEY
(As NICK *seems sunk in thought)*

Dear. . . .

NICK

Oh! Oh, yes . . . I was a . . . quarterback . . . but I was much more . . . adept . . . at boxing, really.

MARTHA
(With great enthusiasm)
BOXING! You hear that, George?

GEORGE *(Resignedly)*

Yes, Martha.

MARTHA
(To NICK*, with peculiar intensity and enthusiasm)*

You musta been pretty good at it . . . I mean, you don't
look like you got hit in the face at all.

HONEY *(Proudly)*

He was intercollegiate state middleweight champion.

NICK *(Embarrassed)*

Honey. . . .

HONEY

Well, you were.

MARTHA

You look like you still got a pretty good body *now*, too
. . . is that right? Have you?

GEORGE *(Intensely)*

Martha . . . decency forbids. . . .

MARTHA
(To GEORGE *. . . still staring at* NICK, *though)*
SHUT UP! *(Now, back to* NICK*)* Well, have you? Have you
kept your body?

NICK
(Unselfconscious . . . almost encouraging her)
It's still pretty good. I work out.

MARTHA *(With a half-smile)*

Do you!

NICK

Yeah.

HONEY

Oh, yes . . . he has a very . . . firm body.

MARTHA
*(Still with that smile . . . a private communica-
tion with* NICK*)*

Have you! Oh, I think that's very nice.

NICK
(Narcissistic, but not directly for MARTHA*)*
Well, you never know . . . *(shrugs)* . . . you know . . .
once you have it. . . .

MARTHA
. . . you never know when it's going to come in handy.

NICK
I was going to say . . . why give it up until you have to.

MARTHA
I couldn't agree with you more.
*(They both smile, and there is a rapport of some
unformed sort established)*
I couldn't agree with you more.

GEORGE
Martha, your obscenity is more than. . . .

MARTHA
George, here, doesn't cotton much to body talk . . . do you
sweetheart? *(No reply)* George isn't too happy when we
get to muscle. You know . . . flat bellies, pectorals. . . .

GEORGE *(To* HONEY*)*
Would you like to take a walk around the garden?

HONEY *(Chiding)*
Oh, now. . . .

GEORGE *(Incredulous)*
You're amused? *(Shrugs)* All right.

MARTHA
Paunchy over there isn't too happy when the conversation

moves to muscle. How much do you weigh?

NICK
A hundred and fifty-five, a hundred and. . . .

MARTHA
Still at the old middleweight limit, eh? That's pretty good.
(*Swings around*) Hey George, tell 'em about the boxing
match *we* had.

GEORGE
(*Slamming his drink down, moving toward the hall*)
Christ!

MARTHA
George! Tell 'em about it!

GEORGE
(*With a sick look on his face*)
You tell them, Martha. You're good at it.
(EXITS)

HONEY
Is he . . . all right?

MARTHA (*Laughs*)
Him? Oh, sure. George and I had this boxing match . . .
Oh, Lord, twenty years ago . . . a couple of years after we
were married.

NICK
A boxing match? The two of you?

HONEY
Really?

MARTHA
Yup . . . the two of us . . . really.

HONEY

(With a little shivery giggle of anticipation)
I can't imagine it.

MARTHA

Well, like I say, it was twenty years ago, and it wasn't in
a ring, or anything like that, you know what I mean. It
was wartime, and Daddy was on this physical fitness
kick . . . Daddy's always admired physical fitness . . .
says a man is only part brain . . . he has a body, too, and
it's his responsibility to keep both of them up . . . you
know?

NICK

Unh-hunh.

MARTHA

Says the brain can't work unless the body's working, too.

NICK

Well, that's not exactly so. . . .

MARTHA

Well, maybe that *isn't* what he says . . . something like it.
But . . . it was wartime, and Daddy got the idea all the
men should learn how to box . . . self-defense. I suppose
the idea was if the Germans landed on the coast, or something, the whole faculty'd go out and punch 'em to death.
. . . I don't know.

NICK

It was probably more the principle of the thing.

MARTHA

No kidding. Anyway, so Daddy had a couple of us over
one Sunday and we went out in the back, and Daddy put
on the gloves himself. Daddy's a strong man. . . . Well,
you know.

NICK

Yes . . . yes.

MARTHA

And he asked George to box with him. Aaaaannnnd . . .
George didn't *want* to . . . probably something about not
wanting to bloody-up his meal ticket. . . .

NICK

Unh-hunh.

MARTHA

. . . Anyway, George said he didn't want to, and Daddy
was saying, "Come on, young man . . . what sort of son-
in-law *are* you?" . . . and stuff like that.

NICK

Yeah.

MARTHA

So, while this was going on . . . I don't know why I *did*
it . . . I got into a pair of gloves myself . . . you know, I
didn't lace 'em up, or anything . . . and I snuck up behind
George, just kidding, and I yelled "Hey George!" and at
the same time I let go sort of a roundhouse right . . . just
kidding, you know?

NICK

Unh-hunh.

MARTHA

. . . and George wheeled around real quick, and he caught
it right in the jaw . . . POW! (NICK laughs) I hadn't meant
it . . . honestly. Anyway . . . POW! Right in the jaw . . .
and he was off balance . . . he must have been . . . and he
stumbled back a few steps, and then, CRASH, he landed
. . . flat . . . in a huckleberry bush!

> (NICK *laughs.* HONEY *goes tsk, tsk, tsk, tsk, and
> shakes her head*)

It was awful, really. It was funny, but it was awful.
*(She thinks, gives a muffled laugh in rueful con-
templation of the incident)*
I think it's colored our whole life. Really I do! It's an ex-
cuse, anyway.
*(GEORGE enters now, his hands behind his back.
No one sees him)*
It's what he uses for being bogged down, anyway . . .
why he hasn't *gone* anywhere.
(GEORGE advances. HONEY sees him)

MARTHA

And it was an *accident* . . . a real, goddamn accident!
*(GEORGE takes from behind his back a short-
barreled shotgun, and calmly aims it at the back
of MARTHA's head. HONEY screams . . . rises. NICK
rises, and, simultaneously, MARTHA turns her
head to face GEORGE. GEORGE pulls the trigger)*

GEORGE

POW!!!
*(Pop! From the barrel of the gun blossoms a
large red and yellow Chinese parasol. HONEY
screams again, this time less, and mostly from relief and confusion)*
You're dead! Pow! You're dead!

NICK *(Laughing)*

Good Lord.
*(HONEY is beside herself. MARTHA laughs too . . .
almost breaks down, her great laugh booming.
GEORGE joins in the general laughter and confusion. It dies, eventually)*

HONEY

Oh! My goodness!

MARTHA *(Joyously)*

Where'd you get that, you bastard?

NICK
(His hand out for the gun)

Let me see that, will you?
(GEORGE hands him the gun)

HONEY

I've never been so frightened in my life! Never!

GEORGE *(A trifle abstracted)*

Oh, I've had it awhile. Did you like that?

MARTHA *(Giggling)*

You bastard.

HONEY *(Wanting attention)*

I've *never* been so frightened . . . never.

NICK

This is quite a gadget.

GEORGE
(Leaning over MARTHA)

You liked that, did you?

MARTHA

Yeah . . . that was pretty good. *(Softer)* C'mon . . . give
me a kiss.

GEORGE
(Indicating NICK and HONEY)

Later, sweetie.
(But MARTHA will not be dissuaded. They kiss,

GEORGE *standing, leaning over* MARTHA'S *chair.*
She takes his hand, places it on her stage-side
breast. He breaks away)

Oh-ho! That's what you're after, is it? What are we going
to have . . . blue games for the guests? Hunh? Hunh?

MARTHA *(Angry-hurt)*

You . . . prick!

GEORGE *(A Pyrrhic victory)*

Everything in its place, Martha . . . everything in its own
good time.

MARTHA
(An unspoken epithet)

You. . . .

GEORGE
(Over to NICK, *who still has the gun)*
Here, let me show you . . . it goes back in, like this.
(Closes the parasol, reinserts it in the gun)

NICK

That's damn clever.

GEORGE *(Puts the gun down)*
Drinks now! Drinks for all!
(Takes NICK's *glass without question . . . goes to* MARTHA*)*

MARTHA *(Still angry-hurt)*

I'm not finished.

HONEY
(As GEORGE *puts out his hand for her glass)*
Oh, I think I need *something.*
(He takes her glass, moves back to the portable bar)

NICK

Is that Japanese?

GEORGE

Probably.

HONEY *(To* MARTHA*)*

I was never so frightened in my life. Weren't you frightened? Just for a second?

MARTHA
(Smothering her rage at GEORGE*)*

I don't remember.

HONEY

Ohhhh, now . . . I bet you were.

GEORGE

Did you really think I was going to kill you, Martha?

MARTHA *(Dripping contempt)*

You? . . . Kill me? . . . That's a laugh.

GEORGE

Well, now, I might . . . some day.

MARTHA

Fat chance.

NICK
(As GEORGE *hands him his drink)*

Where's the john?

GEORGE

Through the hall there . . . and down to your left.

HONEY

Don't you come back with any guns, or anything, now.

NICK *(Laughs)*

Oh, no.

MARTHA

You don't need any props, do you, baby?

NICK

Unh-unh.

MARTHA *(Suggestive)*

I'll bet not. No fake Jap gun for you, eh?

NICK

(Smiles at MARTHA. *Then, to* GEORGE, *indicating a side table near the hall)*

May I leave my drink here?

GEORGE

(As NICK EXITS *without waiting for a reply)*

Yeah ... sure ... why not? We've got half-filled glasses everywhere in the house, wherever Martha forgets she's left them ... in the linen closet, on the edge of the bathtub. ... I even found one in the freezer, once.

MARTHA

(Amused in spite of herself)

You did not!

GEORGE

Yes I did.

MARTHA *(Ibid)*

You did *not!*

GEORGE

(Giving HONEY *her brandy)*

Yes I *did.* *(To* HONEY*)* Brandy doesn't give you a hangover?

HONEY

I never mix. And then, I don't drink very much, either.

GEORGE
(Grimaces behind her back)

Oh . . . that's good. Your . . . your husband was telling me all about the . . . chromosomes.

MARTHA *(Ugly)*

The what?

GEORGE

The chromosomes, Martha . . . the genes, or whatever they are. *(To HONEY)* You've got quite a . . . terrifying husband.

HONEY
(As if she's being joshed)

Ohhhhhhhhh. . . .

GEORGE

No, really. He's quite terrifying, with his chromosomes, and all.

MARTHA

He's in the Math Department.

GEORGE

No, Martha . . . he's a biologist.

MARTHA *(Her voice rising)*

He's in the *Math* Department!

HONEY *(Timidly)*

Uh . . . biology.

MARTHA *(Unconvinced)*

Are *you* sure?

HONEY *(With a little giggle)*

Well, I ought to. *(Then as an afterthought)* Be.

MARTHA *(Grumpy)*

I suppose *so*. I don't know who said he was in the Math Department.

GEORGE

You did, Martha.

MARTHA
(By way of irritable explanation)

Well, I can't be expected to remember *everything*. I meet fifteen new teachers and their goddamn wives . . . present company outlawed, of course . . . *(HONEY nods, smiles sillily)* . . . and I'm supposed to remember *everything*. *(Pause)* So? He's a biologist. Good for him. Biology's even better. It's less . . . abstruse.

GEORGE

Abstract.

MARTHA

ABSTRUSE! In the sense of recondite. *(Sticks her tongue out at GEORGE)* Don't you tell me words. Biology's even better. It's . . . right at the *meat* of things.
(NICK re-enters)
You're right at the meat of things, baby.

NICK
(Taking his drink from the side table)

Oh?

HONEY *(With that giggle)*

They thought you were in the Math Department.

NICK

Well, maybe I ought to be.

MARTHA

You stay right where you are . . . you stay right at the
. . . *meat* of things.

GEORGE

You're obsessed with that phrase, Martha. . . . It's ugly.

MARTHA
(Ignoring GEORGE *. . . to* NICK*)*
You stay right there. *(Laughs)* Hell, you can take over
the History Department just as easy from there as any-
where else. God knows, *some*body's going to take over the
History Department, *some* day, and it ain't going to be
Georgie-boy, there . . . that's for sure. Are ya, swampy . . .
are ya, hunh?

GEORGE

In my mind, Martha, you are buried in cement, right up
to your neck. (MARTHA *giggles*) No . . . right up to your
nose . . . that's much quieter.

MARTHA *(To* NICK*)*
Georgie-boy, here, says you're terrifying. Why are you
terrifying?

NICK *(With a small smile)*
I didn't know I was.

HONEY *(A little thickly)*
It's because of your chromosomes, dear.

NICK
Oh, the chromosome business. . . .

MARTHA *(To* NICK*)*
What's all this about chromosomes?

NICK
Well, chromosomes are. . . .

MARTHA

I know what chromosomes are, sweetie, I love 'em.

NICK

Oh. . . . Well, then.

GEORGE

Martha eats them . . . for breakfast . . . she sprinkles them on her cereal. (*To* MARTHA, *now*) It's very simple, Martha, this young man is working on a system whereby chromosomes can be altered . . . well not all by himself —he probably has one or two co-conspirators—the genetic makeup of a sperm cell changed, reordered . . . *to* order, actually . . . for hair and eye color, stature, potency . . . I imagine . . . hairiness, features, health . . . and *mind*. Most important . . . Mind. All imbalances will be corrected, sifted out . . . propensity for various diseases will be gone, longevity assured. We will have a race of men . . . test-tube-bred . . . incubator-born . . . superb and sublime.

MARTHA (*Impressed*)

Hunh!

HONEY

How exciting!

GEORGE

But! Everyone will tend to be rather the same. . . . Alike. Everyone . . . and I'm sure I'm not wrong here . . . will tend to look like this young man *here*.

MARTHA

That's not a bad idea.

NICK (*Impatient*)

All right, now. . . .

GEORGE

It will, on the surface of it, be all rather pretty . . . quite
jolly. But of course there will be a dank side to it, too. A
certain amount of regulation will be necessary . . . uh . . .
for the experiment to succeed. A certain number of sperm
tubes will have to be cut.

MARTHA

Hunh! . . .

GEORGE

Millions upon millions of them . . . millions of tiny little
slicing operations that will leave just the smallest scar, on
the underside of the scrotum (MARTHA *laughs*) but which
will assure the sterility of the imperfect . . . the ugly,
the stupid . . . the . . . unfit.

NICK (*Grimly*)

Now look . . . !

GEORGE

. . . with this, we will have, in time, a race of glorious men.

MARTHA

Hunh!

GEORGE

I suspect we will not have much music, much painting,
but we will have a civilization of men, smooth, blond, and
right at the middleweight limit.

MARTHA

Awww. . . .

GEORGE

. . . a race of scientists and mathematicians, each dedi-
cated to and working for the greater glory of the super-
civilization.

MARTHA

Goody.

GEORGE

There will be a certain . . . loss of liberty, I imagine, as a result of this experiment . . . but diversity will no longer be the goal. Cultures and races will eventually vanish . . . the ants will take over the world.

NICK

Are you finished?

GEORGE *(Ignoring him)*

And I, naturally, am rather opposed to all this. History, which is my field . . . history, of which I am one of the most famous bogs. . . .

MARTHA

Ha, ha, HA!

GEORGE

. . . will lose its glorious variety and unpredictability. I, and with me the . . . the surprise, the multiplexity, the sea-changing rhythm of . . . history, will be eliminated. There will be order and constancy . . . and I am unalterably opposed to it. I will not give up Berlin!

MARTHA

You'll give up Berlin, sweetheart. You going to defend it with your paunch?

HONEY

I don't see what Berlin has to *do* with anything.

GEORGE

There is a saloon in West Berlin where the barstools are five feet high. And the earth . . . the floor . . . is so . . .

far . . . below you. I will not give up things like that. No
. . . I won't. I will fight you, young man . . . one hand on
my scrotum, to be sure . . . but with my free hand I will
battle you to the death.

MARTHA *(Mocking, laughing)*

Bravo!

NICK *(To* GEORGE*)*

That's right. And I am going to be the wave of the future.

MARTHA

You bet you are, baby.

HONEY *(Quite drunk—to* NICK*)*

I don't see why you want to do all those things, dear. You
never told me.

NICK *(Angry)*

Oh for God's sake!

HONEY *(Shocked)*

OH!

GEORGE

The most profound indication of a social malignancy . . .
no sense of humor. None of the monoliths could take a
joke. Read history. I know something about history.

NICK

(To GEORGE, *trying to make light of it all)*

You . . . you don't know much about science, do you?

GEORGE

I know something about history. I know when I'm being
threatened.

MARTHA *(Salaciously—to* NICK*)*

So, everyone's going to look like you, eh?

NICK

Oh, sure. I'm going to be a personal screwing machine!

MARTHA

Isn't that nice.

HONEY
(Her hands over her ears)

Dear, you mustn't . . . you mustn't . . . you mustn't.

NICK *(Impatiently)*

I'm sorry, Honey.

HONEY

Such language. It's. . . .

NICK

I'm *sorry*. All right?

HONEY *(Pouting)*

Well . . . all right. *(Suddenly she giggles insanely, subsides. To* GEORGE*)* . . . When is your son? *(Giggles again)*

GEORGE

What?

NICK *(Distastefully)*

Something about your son.

GEORGE

SON!

HONEY

When is . . . where is your son . . . coming home? *(Giggles)*

GEORGE

Ohhhh. *(Too formal)* Martha? When is our son coming home?

MARTHA

Never mind.

GEORGE

No, no . . . I want to know . . . you brought it out into the open. When is he coming home, Martha?

MARTHA

I said never mind. I'm sorry I brought it up.

GEORGE

Him up . . . not it. You brought *him* up. Well, more or less. When's the little bugger going to appear, hunh? I mean isn't tomorrow meant to be his birthday, or something?

MARTHA

I don't want to talk about it!

GEORGE *(Falsely innocent)*

But Martha. . . .

MARTHA

I DON'T WANT TO TALK ABOUT IT!

GEORGE

I'll bet you don't. *(To* HONEY *and* NICK) Martha does not want to talk about it . . . him. Martha is sorry she brought it up . . . him.

HONEY *(Idiotically)*

When's the little bugger coming home? *(Giggles)*

GEORGE

Yes, Martha . . . since you had the bad taste to bring the matter up in the first place . . . when *is* the little bugger coming home?

NICK

Honey, do you think you . . . ?

MARTHA

George talks disparagingly about the little bugger because . . . well, because he has problems.

GEORGE

The little bugger has problems? What problems has the
little bugger got?

MARTHA

Not the little bugger . . . stop calling him that! You!
You've got problems.

GEORGE *(Feigned disdain)*

I've never heard of anything more ridiculous in my life.

HONEY

Neither have I!

NICK

Honey. . . .

MARTHA

George's biggest problem about the little . . . ha, ha, ha,
HA! . . . about our son, about our great big son, is that
deep down in the private-most pit of his gut, he's not
completely sure it's his own kid.

GEORGE *(Deeply serious)*

My God, you're a wicked woman.

MARTHA

And I've told you a million times, baby . . . I wouldn't
conceive with anyone but you . . . you know that, baby.

GEORGE

A deeply wicked person.

HONEY *(Deep in drunken grief)*

My, my, my, my. Oh, my.

NICK

I'm not sure that this is a subject for. . . .

GEORGE

Martha's lying. I want you to know that, right now. Martha's lying. (MARTHA *laughs*) There are very few things in this world that I *am* sure of . . . national boundaries, the level of the ocean, political allegiances, practical morality . . . none of these would I stake my stick on any more . . . but the one thing in this whole sinking world that I am sure of is my partnership, my chromosomological partnership in the . . . creation of our . . . blond-eyed, blue-haired . . . son.

HONEY

Oh, I'm so glad!

MARTHA

That was a very pretty speech, George.

GEORGE

Thank you, Martha.

MARTHA

You rose to the occasion . . . good. Real good.

HONEY

Well . . . real well.

NICK

Honey. . . .

GEORGE

Martha knows . . . she knows better.

MARTHA *(Proudly)*

I know better. I been to college like everybody else.

GEORGE

Martha been to college. Martha been to a convent when she were a little twig of a thing, too.

MARTHA

And I was an atheist. *(Uncertainly)* I still am.

GEORGE

Not an atheist, Martha . . . a pagan. *(To* HONEY *and* NICK*)* Martha is the only true pagan on the eastern seaboard. *(*MARTHA *laughs)*

HONEY

Oh, that's nice. Isn't that nice, dear?

NICK *(Humoring her)*

Yes . . . wonderful.

GEORGE

And Martha paints blue circles around her things.

NICK

You do?

MARTHA
    (Defensively, for the joke's sake)
Sometimes. *(Beckoning)* You wanna see?

GEORGE *(Admonishing)*

Tut, tut, tut.

MARTHA

Tut, tut yourself . . . you old floozie!

HONEY

He's not a floozie . . . he can't be a floozie . . . you're a
floozie.

(Giggles)

MARTHA
(Shaking a finger at HONEY)
Now you watch yourself!

HONEY *(Cheerfully)*
All right. I'd like a nipper of brandy, please.

NICK
Honey, I think you've had enough, now. . . .

GEORGE
Nonsense! Everybody's ready, I think. *(Takes glasses, etc.)*

HONEY *(Echoing GEORGE)*
Nonsense.

NICK *(Shrugging)*
O.K.

MARTHA *(To GEORGE)*
Our son does *not* have blue hair . . . or blue eyes, for that
matter. He has green eyes . . . like me.

GEORGE
He has blue eyes, Martha.

MARTHA *(Determined)*
Green.

GEORGE *(Patronizing)*
Blue, Martha.

MARTHA *(Ugly)*

GREEN! *(To* HONEY *and* NICK*)* He has the loveliest green eyes . . . they aren't all flaked with brown and gray, you know . . . hazel . . . they're real green . . . deep, pure green eyes . . . like mine.

NICK *(Peers)*

Your eyes are . . . brown, aren't they?

MARTHA

Green! *(A little too fast)* Well, in some lights they *look* brown, but they're green. Not green like his . . . more hazel. George has watery blue eyes . . . milky blue.

GEORGE

Make up your mind, Martha.

MARTHA

I was giving you the benefit of the doubt. *(Now back to the others)* Daddy has green eyes, too.

GEORGE

He does not! Your father has tiny red eyes . . . like a white mouse. In fact, he *is* a white mouse.

MARTHA

You wouldn't dare say a thing like that if he was here! You're a coward!

GEORGE *(To* HONEY *and* NICK*)*

You know . . . that great shock of white hair, and those little beady red eyes . . . a great big white mouse.

MARTHA

George hates Daddy . . . not for anything Daddy's done

to him, but for his own. . . .

> GEORGE
> *(Nodding . . . finishing it for her)*

. . . inadequacies.

> MARTHA *(Cheerfully)*

That's right. You hit it . . . right on the snout. *(Seeing GEORGE EXITING)* Where do you think *you're* going?

> GEORGE

We need some more booze, angel.

> MARTHA

Oh. *(Pause)* So, go.

> GEORGE *(Exiting)*

Thank you.

> MARTHA
> *(Seeing that GEORGE has gone)*

He's a good bartender . . . a good bar nurse. The S.O.B., he hates my father. You know that?

> NICK
> *(Trying to make light of it)*

Oh, come on.

> MARTHA *(Offended)*

You think I'm kidding? You think I'm joking? I never joke . . . I don't have a sense of humor. *(Almost pouting)* I have a fine sense of the ridiculous, but no sense of humor. *(Affirmatively)* I have no sense of humor!

> HONEY *(Happily)*

I haven't, either.

NICK *(Half-heartedly)*

Yes, you have, Honey . . . a quiet one.

HONEY *(Proudly)*

Thank you.

MARTHA

You want to know *why* the S.O.B. hates my father? You want me to tell you? All right. . . . I will now tell you why the S.O.B. hates my father.

HONEY
        (Swinging to some sort of attention)

Oh, good!

MARTHA *(Sternly, to* HONEY*)*

Some people feed on the calamities of others.

HONEY *(Offended)*

They do not!

NICK

Honey. . . .

MARTHA

All right! Shut up! Both of you! *(Pause)* All right, now. Mommy died early, see, and I sort of grew up with Daddy. *(Pause—thinks)* . . . I went away to school, and stuff, but I more or less grew up with him. Jesus, I admired that guy! I worshipped him . . . I absolutely worshipped him. I still do. And he was pretty fond of me, too . . . you know? We had a real . . . rapport going . . . a real rapport.

NICK

Yeah, yeah.

MARTHA

And Daddy built this college . . . I mean, he built it up

from what it was . . . it's his whole life. He *is* the college.

NICK

Unh-hunh.

MARTHA

The college is him. You know what the endowment was
when he took over, and what it is *now?* You look it up
some time.

NICK

I know . . . I read about it. . . .

MARTHA

Shut up and listen . . . *(As an afterthought)* . . . cutie.
So after I got done with college and stuff, I came back
here and sort of . . . sat around, for a while. I wasn't
married, or anything. Wellllll, I'd *been* married . . . sort
of . . . for a week, my sophomore year at Miss Muff's
Academy for Young Ladies . . . college. A kind of junior
Lady Chatterley arrangement, as it turned out . . . the
marriage. *(NICK laughs)* He mowed the lawn at Miss
Muff's, sitting up there, all naked, on a big power mower,
mowing away. But Daddy and Miss Muff got together
and put an end to that . . . real quick . . . annulled . . .
which is a laugh . . . because theoretically you can't get
an annullment if there's entrance. Ha! Anyway, so I was
revirginized, finished at Miss Muff's . . . where they had
one less gardener's boy, and a real shame, that was . . .
and I came back here and sort of sat around for a while.
I was hostess for Daddy and I took care of him . . . and
it was . . . nice. It was very nice.

NICK

Yes . . . yes.

MARTHA

What do you mean, yes, yes? How would you know?

(NICK *shrugs helplessly*)

Lover.

(NICK *smiles a little*)

And I got the idea, about then, that I'd marry into the college . . . which didn't seem to be quite as stupid as it turned out. I mean, Daddy had a sense of history . . . of . . . continuation. . . . Why don't you come over here and sit by me?

NICK

(*Indicating* HONEY, *who is barely with it*)

I . . . don't think I . . . should. . . . I . . . .

MARTHA

Suit yourself. A sense of continuation . . . history . . . and he'd always had it in the back of his mind to . . . *groom* someone to take over . . . some time, when he quit. A succession . . . you know what I mean?

NICK

Yes, I do.

MARTHA

Which is natural enough. When you've made something, you want to pass it on, to somebody. So, I was sort of on the lookout, for . . . prospects with the new men. An heir-apparent. (*Laughs*) It wasn't *Daddy's* idea that I had to necessarily marry the guy. I mean, I wasn't the alba-tross . . . you didn't have to take me to get the prize, or anything like that. It was something *I* had in the back of *my* mind. And a lot of the new men were married . . . naturally.

NICK

Sure.

MARTHA
(With a strange smile)

Like you, baby.

HONEY *(A mindless echo)*

Like you, baby.

MARTHA *(Ironically)*

But then George came along . . . along come George.

GEORGE
(Re-entering, with liquor)

And along came George, bearing hooch. What are you doing now, Martha?

MARTHA *(Unfazed)*

I'm telling a story. Sit down . . . you'll learn something.

GEORGE
(Stays standing. Puts the liquor on the portable bar)

All rightie.

HONEY

You've come back!

GEORGE

That's right.

HONEY

Dear! He's come back!

NICK

Yes, I see . . . I see.

MARTHA

Where was I?

HONEY

I'm *so* glad.

NICK

Shhhhh.

HONEY *(Imitating him)*

Shhhhh.

MARTHA

Oh yeah. And along came George. That's right. Who was young . . . intelligent . . . and . . . bushy-tailed, and . . . sort of cute . . . if you can imagine it. . . .

GEORGE

. . . and younger than you. . . .

MARTHA

. . . and younger than me. . . .

GEORGE

. . . by six years. . . .

MARTHA

. . . by six years. . . . It doesn't bother me, George. . . . And along he came, bright-eyed, into the History Department. And you know what I did, dumb cluck that I am? You know what I did? I fell for him.

HONEY *(Dreamy)*

Oh, that's nice.

GEORGE

Yes, she did. You should have seen it. She'd sit outside of my room, on the lawn, at night, and she'd howl and claw at the turf . . . I couldn't work.

MARTHA
(Laughs, really amused)
I actually fell for him . . . it . . . that, there.

GEORGE

Martha's a Romantic at heart.

MARTHA

That I am. So, I actually fell for him. And the match
seemed . . . practical, too. You know, Daddy was looking
for someone to. . . .

GEORGE

Just a minute, Martha. . . .

MARTHA

. . . take over, some time, when he was ready to. . . .

GEORGE *(Stony)*

Just a minute, Martha.

MARTHA

. . . retire, and so I thought. . . .

GEORGE

STOP IT, MARTHA!

MARTHA *(Irritated)*

Whadda you want?

GEORGE *(Too patiently)*

I'd thought you were telling the story of our courtship,
Martha . . . I didn't know you were going to start in on
the other business.

MARTHA *(So-thereish)*

Well, I am!

GEORGE

I wouldn't, if I were you.

MARTHA

Oh . . . you wouldn't? Well, you're not!

GEORGE

Now, you've already sprung a leak about you-know-what. . . .

MARTHA *(A duck)*

What? What?

GEORGE

. . . about the apple of our eye . . . the sprout . . . the little bugger . . . *(spits it out)* . . . our *son* . . . and if you start in on this other business, I warn you, Martha, it's going to make me angry.

MARTHA *(Laughing at him)*

Oh, it is, is it?

GEORGE

I warn you.

MARTHA *(Incredulous)*

You *what?*

GEORGE *(Very quietly)*

I warn you.

NICK

Do you really think we have to go through . . . ?

MARTHA

I stand warned! *(Pause . . . then, to* HONEY *and* NICK*)* So, anyway, I married the S.O.B., and I had it all planned out. . . . He was the groom . . . he was going to be groomed. He'd take over some day . . . first, he'd take

over the History Department, and then, when Daddy
retired, he'd take over the college . . . you know? That's
the way it was supposed to be.

(To GEORGE, *who is at the portable bar with his
back to her)*

You getting angry, baby? Hunh? *(Now back)* That's the
way it was *supposed* to be. Very simple. And Daddy
seemed to think it was a pretty good idea, too. For a
while. Until he watched for a couple of years! *(To* GEORGE
again) You getting angrier? *(Now back)* Until he watched
for a couple of years and started thinking maybe it wasn't
such a good idea after all . . . that maybe Georgie-boy
didn't have the *stuff* . . . that he didn't have it in him!

                        GEORGE
              (Still with his back to them all)
Stop it, Martha.

                        MARTHA *(Viciously triumphant)*
The hell I will! You see, George didn't have much . . .
push . . . he wasn't particularly . . . aggressive. In fact he
was sort of a . . . *(Spits the word at* GEORGE's *back)* . . . a
FLOP! A great . . . big . . . fat . . . FLOP!

*(*CRASH! *Immediately after* FLOP! GEORGE *breaks a
bottle against the portable bar and stands there, still
with his back to them all, holding the remains of
the bottle by the neck. There is a silence, with
everyone frozen. Then. . . .)*

                        GEORGE *(Almost crying)*
I said stop, Martha.

                        MARTHA
              (After considering what course to take)
I hope that was an empty bottle, George. You don't want
to waste good liquor . . . not on your salary.

(GEORGE *drops the broken bottle on the floor, not moving*)

Not on an Associate Professor's salary. (*To* NICK *and* HONEY) I mean, he'd be . . . no good . . . at trustees' dinners, fund raising. He didn't have any . . . personality, you know what I mean? Which was disappointing to Daddy, as you can imagine. So, here I am, stuck with this flop. . . .

GEORGE (*Turning around*)

. . . don't go on, Martha. . . .

MARTHA

. . . this BOG in the History Department. . . .

GEORGE

. . . don't, Martha, don't. . . .

MARTHA	GEORGE
(*Her voice rising to match his*)	(*Under her, then covering, to drown her*)
. . . who's married to the President's daughter, who's expected to *be* somebody, not just some nobody, some bookworm, somebody who's so damn . . . contemplative, he can't make anything out of himself, somebody without the *guts* to make anybody proud of him . . . ALL RIGHT, GEORGE!	I said, don't. All right . . . all right: (*Sings*) Who's afraid of Virginia Woolf, Virginia Woolf, Virginia Woolf, Who's afraid of Virginia Woolf, early in the morning.

GEORGE *and* HONEY
(Who joins him drunkenly)
Who's afraid of Virginia Woolf,
                    Virginia Woolf,
                    Virginia Woolf . . . *(etc.)*

MARTHA

STOP IT!

(A brief silence)

HONEY
(Rising, moving toward the hall)
I'm going to be sick . . . I'm going to be sick . . . I'm
going to vomit.

(EXITS)

NICK *(Going after her)*
Oh, for God's sake!

(EXITS)

MARTHA
(Going after them, looks back at GEORGE, *contemptuously)*
Jesus! *(EXITS.* GEORGE *is alone on stage)*

CURTAIN

ACT TWO

WALPURGISNACHT

GEORGE, *by himself:* NICK *re-enters.*

NICK *(After a silence)*

I . . . guess . . . she's all right. *(No answer)* She . . . really shouldn't drink. *(No answer)* She's . . . frail. *(No answer)* Uh . . . slim-hipped, as you'd have it. (GEORGE *smiles vaguely)* I'm really very sorry.

GEORGE *(Quietly)*

Where's my little yum yum? Where's Martha?

NICK

She's making coffee . . . in the kitchen. She . . . gets sick quite easily.

GEORGE *(Preoccupied)*

Martha? Oh no, Martha hasn't been sick a day in her life, unless you count the time she spends in the rest home. . . .

NICK *(He, too, quietly)*

No, no; *my* wife . . . *my* wife gets sick quite easily. Your wife is Martha.

GEORGE *(With some rue)*

Oh, yes . . . I know.

NICK *(A statement of fact)*

She doesn't really spend any time in a rest home.

GEORGE

Your wife?

NICK

No. Yours.

GEORGE

Oh! Mine. *(Pause)* No, no, she doesn't . . . *I* would; I mean if I were . . . her . . . she . . . *I* would. But I'm not . . . and so I don't. *(Pause)* I'd like to, though. It gets pretty bouncy around here sometimes.

NICK *(Coolly)*

Yes . . . I'm sure.

GEORGE

Well, you saw an example of it.

NICK

I try not to. . . .

GEORGE

Get involved. Um? Isn't that right?

NICK

Yes . . . that's right.

GEORGE

I'd imagine not.

NICK

I find it . . . embarrassing.

GEORGE *(Sarcastic)*

Oh, you do, hunh?

NICK

Yes. Really. Quite.

GEORGE *(Mimicking him)*

Yes. Really. Quite. *(Then aloud, but to himself)* IT'S DIS-GUSTING!

NICK

Now look! I didn't have anything. . . .

GEORGE

DISGUSTING! *(Quietly, but with great intensity)* Do you think I like having that . . . whatever-it-is . . . ridiculing me, tearing me down, in front of . . . *(Waves his hand in a gesture of contemptuous dismissal)* YOU? Do you think I *care* for it?

NICK *(Cold—unfriendly)*

Well, no . . . I don't imagine you care for it at all.

GEORGE

Oh, you don't imagine it, hunh?

NICK *(Antagonistic)*

No . . . I don't. I don't imagine you do!

GEORGE *(Withering)*

Your sympathy disarms me . . . your . . . your compassion makes me weep! Large, salty, unscientific tears!

NICK *(With great disdain)*

I just don't see why you feel you have to subject *other* people to it.

GEORGE

I?

NICK

If you and your . . . wife . . . want to go at each other, like a couple of. . . .

GEORGE

I! Why I want to!

NICK

. . . animals, I don't see why you don't do it when there
aren't any. . . .

GEORGE

(Laughing through his anger)
Why, you smug, self-righteous little. . . .

NICK *(A genuine threat)*

CAN . . . IT . . . MISTER!

(Silence)

Just . . . watch it!

GEORGE

. . . scientist.

NICK

I've never hit an older man.

GEORGE *(Considers it)*

Oh. *(Pause)* You just hit younger men . . . and children
. . . women . . . birds. *(Sees that NICK is not amused)*
Well, you're quite right, of course. It isn't the prettiest
spectacle . . . seeing a couple of middle-age types hacking
away at each other, all red in the face and winded, miss-
ing half the time.

NICK

Oh, you two don't miss . . . you two are pretty good. Impressive.

GEORGE

And impressive things impress you, don't they? You're . . .
easily impressed . . . sort of a . . . pragmatic idealism.

NICK *(A tight smile)*

No, it's that sometimes I can admire things that I don't

admire. Now, flagellation isn't my idea of good times, but. . . .

GEORGE

. . . but you can admire a good flagellator . . . a real pro.

NICK

Unh-hunh . . . yeah.

GEORGE

Your wife throws up a lot, eh?

NICK

I didn't say that. . . . I said she gets sick quite easily.

GEORGE

Oh. I thought by sick you meant. . . .

NICK

Well, it's true. . . . She . . . she does throw up a lot. Once she starts . . . there's practically no stopping her. . . . I mean, she'll go right on . . . for hours. Not all the time, but . . . regularly.

GEORGE

You can tell time by her, hunh?

NICK

Just about.

GEORGE

Drink?

NICK

Sure. (*With no emotion, except the faintest distaste, as* GEORGE *takes his glass to the bar*) I married her because she was pregnant.

GEORGE

(*Pause*) Oh? (*Pause*) But you said you didn't have any

children. . . . When I asked you, you said. . . .

NICK

She wasn't . . . really. It was a hysterical pregnancy. She
blew up, and then she went down.

GEORGE

And while she was up, you married her.

NICK

And then she went down.
*(They both laugh, and are a little surprised that
they do)*

GEORGE

Uh . . . Bourbon *is* right.

NICK

Uh . . . yes, Bourbon.

GEORGE *(At the bar, still)*

When I was sixteen and going to prep school, during the
Punic Wars, a bunch of us used to go into New York on
the first day of vacations, before we fanned out to our
homes, and in the evening this bunch of us used to go to
this gin mill owned by the gangster-father of one of us
—for this was during the Great Experiment, or Prohibi-
tion, as it is more frequently called, and it was a bad
time for the liquor lobby, but a fine time for the crooks
and the cops—and we would go to this gin mill, and we
would drink with the grown-ups and listen to the jazz.
And one time, in the bunch of us, there was this boy
who was fifteen, and he had killed his mother with a shotgun some years before—accidentally, completely accidentally, without even an unconscious motivation, I have no
doubt, no doubt at all—and this one evening this boy went
with us, and we ordered our drinks, and when it came

his turn he said, I'll have bergin . . . give me some bergin, please . . . bergin and water. Well, we all laughed . . . he was blond and he had the face of a cherub, and we all laughed, and his cheeks went red and the color rose in his neck, and the assistant crook who had taken our order told people at the next table what the boy had said, and then they laughed, and then more people were told and the laughter grew, and more people and more laughter, and no one was laughing more than us, and none of us more than the boy who had shot his mother. And soon, everyone in the gin mill knew what the laughter was about, and everyone started ordering bergin, and laughing when they ordered it. And soon, of course, the laughter became less general, but it did not subside, entirely, for a very long time, for always at this table or that someone would order bergin and a new area of laughter would rise. We drank free that night, and we were bought champagne by the management, by the gangster-father of one of us. And, of course, we suffered the next day, each of us, alone, on his train, away from New York, each of us with a grown-up's hangover . . . but it was the grandest day of my . . . youth.

(*Hands* NICK *a drink on the word*)

NICK (*Very quietly*)

Thank you. What . . . what happened to the boy . . . the boy who had shot his mother?

GEORGE

I won't tell you.

NICK

All right.

GEORGE

The following summer, on a country road, with his

learner's permit in his pocket and his father on the front
seat to his right, he swerved the car, to avoid a porcupine,
and drove straight into a large tree.

NICK *(Faintly pleading)*

No.

GEORGE

He was not killed, of course. And in the hospital, when he
was conscious and out of danger, and when they told him
that his father *was* dead, he began to laugh, I have been
told, and his laughter grew and he would not stop, and it
was not until after they jammed a needle in his arm, not
until after that, until his consciousness slipped away from
him, that his laughter subsided . . . stopped. And when
he was recovered from his injuries enough so that he
could be moved without damage should he struggle, he
was put in an asylum. That was thirty years ago.

NICK

Is he . . . still there?

GEORGE

Oh, yes. And I'm told that for these thirty years he has
. . . not . . . uttered . . . one . . . sound.

(A rather long silence: five seconds, please)
MARTHA! *(Pause)* MARTHA!

NICK

I told you . . . she's making coffee.

GEORGE

For your hysterical wife, who goes up and down.

NICK

Went. Up and down.

GEORGE

Went. No more?

NICK

No more. Nothing.

GEORGE
(After a sympathetic pause)

The saddest thing about men. . . . Well, no, one of the saddest things about men is the way they age . . . some of them. Do you know what it is with insane people? Do you? . . . the quiet ones?

NICK

No.

GEORGE

They don't change . . . they don't grow old.

NICK

They must.

GEORGE

Well, eventually, probably, yes. But they don't . . . in the usual sense. They maintain a . . . a firm-skinned serenity . . . the . . . the under-use of everything leaves them . . . quite whole.

NICK

Are you recommending it?

GEORGE

No. Some things are sad, though. *(Imitates a pep-talker)* But ya jest gotta buck up an' face 'em, 'at's all. Buck up! *(Pause)* Martha doesn't have hysterical pregnancies.

NICK

My wife had *one*.

GEORGE

Yes. Martha doesn't have pregnancies at all.

NICK

Well, no . . . I don't imagine so . . . now. Do you have any
other kids? Do you have any daughters, or anything?

GEORGE
(As if it's a great joke)
Do we have any *what?*

NICK

Do you have any . . . I mean, do you have only one . . .
kid . . . uh . . . your son?

GEORGE
(With a private knowledge)
Oh no . . . just one . . . one boy . . . our son.

NICK

Well . . . *(Shrugs)* . . . that's nice.

GEORGE

Oh ho, ho. Yes, well, he's a . . . comfort, a bean bag.

NICK

A what?

GEORGE

A bean bag. Bean bag. You wouldn't understand. *(Over-
distinct)* Bean . . . bag.

NICK

I *heard* you . . . I didn't say I was deaf . . . I said I didn't
understand.

GEORGE

You didn't say that at all.

NICK

I meant I was *implying* I didn't understand. *(Under his
breath)* For Christ's sake!

GEORGE

You're getting testy.

NICK *(Testy)*

I'm sorry.

GEORGE

All I said was, our son . . . the apple of our three eyes, Martha being a Cyclops . . . our son is a bean bag, and you get testy.

NICK

I'm sorry! It's late, I'm tired, I've been drinking since nine o'clock, my wife is vomiting, there's been a lot of screaming going on around here. . . .

GEORGE

And so you're testy. Naturally. Don't . . . worry about it. Anybody who comes here ends up getting . . . testy. It's expected . . . don't be upset.

NICK *(Testy)*

I'm not upset!

GEORGE

You're testy.

NICK

Yes.

GEORGE

I'd like to set you straight about something . . . while the little ladies are out of the room . . . I'd like to set you straight about what Martha said.

NICK

I don't . . . make judgments, so there's no need, really, unless you. . . .

GEORGE

Well, I want to. I know you don't like to become involved
. . . I know you like to . . . preserve your scientific de-
tachment in the face of—for lack of a better word—Life
. . . and all . . . but still, I want to tell you.

NICK *(A tight, formal smile)*

I'm a . . . guest. You go right ahead.

GEORGE
(Mocking appreciation)

Oh . . . well, thanks. Now! That makes me feel all warm
and runny inside.

NICK

Well, if you're going to . . .

MARTHA'S VOICE

HEY!

NICK

. . . if you're going to start that kind of stuff again. . . .

GEORGE

Hark! Forest sounds.

NICK

Hm?

GEORGE

Animal noises.

MARTHA *(Sticking her head in)*

Hey!

NICK

Oh!

GEORGE

Well, here's nursie.

MARTHA *(To* NICK*)*

We're sitting up . . . we're having coffee, and we'll be
back in.

NICK *(Not rising)*

Oh . . . is there anything I should do?

MARTHA

Nayh. You just stay here and listen to George's side of
things. Bore yourself to death.

GEORGE

Monstre!

MARTHA

Cochon!

GEORGE

Bête!

MARTHA

Canaille!

GEORGE

Putain!

MARTHA
(With a gesture of contemptuous dismissal)

Yaaaahhhh! You two types amuse yourselves . . . we'll be
in. *(As she goes)* You clean up the mess you made,
George?

GEORGE
*(*MARTHA *goes.* GEORGE *speaks to the empty hallway)*

No, Martha, I did not clean up the mess I made. I've been

trying for years to clean up the mess I made.

NICK

Have you?

GEORGE

Hm?

NICK

Have you been trying for years?

GEORGE

(After a long pause . . . looking at him)
Accommodation, malleability, adjustment . . . those do
seem to be in the order of things, don't they?

NICK

Don't try to put me in the same class with you!

GEORGE

(Pause) Oh. *(Pause)* No, of course not. Things are simpler
with you . . . you marry a woman because she's all blown
up . . . while I, in my clumsy, old-fashioned way. . . .

NICK

There was more to it than that!

GEORGE

Sure! I'll bet she has money, too!

NICK

(Looks hurt. Then, determined, after a pause)
Yes.

GEORGE

Yes? *(Joyfully)* YES! You mean I was right? I hit it?

NICK

Well, you see. . . .

GEORGE

My God, what archery! First try, too. How about that!

NICK

You see. . . .

GEORGE

There were other things.

NICK

Yes.

GEORGE

To compensate.

NICK

Yes.

GEORGE

There always are. (*Sees that* NICK *is reacting badly*) No, I'm sure there are. I didn't mean to be . . . flip. There are *always* compensating factors . . . as in the case of Martha and myself. . . . Now, on the surface of it. . . .

NICK

We sort of grew up together, you know. . . .

GEORGE

. . . it looks to be a kind of knock-about, drag-out affair, on the *surface* of it. . . .

NICK

We knew each other from, oh God, I don't know, when we were *six*, or something. . . .

GEORGE

. . . but somewhere back there, at the beginning of it,
right when I first came to New Carthage, back then. . . .

NICK *(With some irritation)*

I'm *sorry.*

GEORGE

Hm? Oh. No, no . . . *I'm* sorry.

NICK

No . . . it's . . . it's all right.

GEORGE

No . . . you go ahead.

NICK

No . . . please.

GEORGE

I insist. . . . You're a guest. You go first.

NICK

Well, it seems a little silly . . . now.

GEORGE

Nonsense! *(Pause)* But if you were six, she must have
been four, or something.

NICK

Maybe I was eight . . . she was six. We . . . we used to
play . . . doctor.

GEORGE

That's a good healthy heterosexual beginning.

NICK *(Laughing)*

Yup.

GEORGE

The scientist even then, eh?

NICK *(Laughs)*

Yeah. And it was . . . always taken for granted . . . you know . . . by our families, and by us, too, I guess. And . . . so, we did.

GEORGE

(Pause) Did what?

NICK

We got married.

GEORGE

When you were eight?

NICK

No. No, of course not. Much later.

GEORGE

I wondered.

NICK

I wouldn't say there was any . . . particular *passion* between us, even at the beginning . . . of our marriage, I mean.

GEORGE

Well, certainly no surprise, no earth-shaking discoveries, after Doctor, and all.

NICK *(Uncertainly)*

No. . . .

GEORGE

Everything's all pretty much the same, anyway . . . in *spite* of what they say about Chinese women.

NICK

What is that?

GEORGE

Let me freshen you up. *(Takes* NICK's *glass)*

NICK

Oh, thanks. After a while you don't get any drunker, do you?

GEORGE

Well, you *do* . . . but it's different . . . everything slows down. . . . you get sodden. . . . unless you can up-chuck . . . like your wife . . . then you can sort of start all over again.

NICK

Everybody drinks a lot here in the East. *(Thinks about it)* Everybody drinks a lot in the Middle West, too.

GEORGE

We drink a great deal in this country, and I suspect we'll be drinking a great deal more, too . . . if we survive. We should be Arabs or Italians . . . the Arabs don't drink, and the Italians don't get drunk much, except on religious holidays. We should live on Crete, or something.

NICK

(Sarcastically . . . as if killing a joke)
And that, of course, would make us cretins.

GEORGE *(Mild surprise)*

So it would. *(Hands* NICK *his drink)* Tell me about your wife's money.

NICK *(Suddenly suspicious)*

Why?

GEORGE

Well . . . don't, then.

NICK

What do you want to know about my wife's money for?
(*Ugly*) Hunh?

GEORGE

Well, I thought it would be nice.

NICK

No you didn't.

GEORGE

(*Still deceptively bland*)

All right. . . . I want to know about your wife's money because . . . well, because I'm fascinated by the method-
ology . . . by the pragmatic accommodation by which you
wave-of-the-future boys are going to take over.

NICK

You're starting in again.

GEORGE

Am I? No I'm not. Look . . . Martha has money too. I
mean, her father's been robbing this place blind for years,
and. . . .

NICK

No, he hasn't. He has not.

GEORGE

He hasn't?

NICK

No.

GEORGE *(Shrugs)*

Very well. . . . Martha's father has *not* been robbing this place blind for years, and Martha does not have any money. O.K.?

NICK

We were talking about *my* wife's money . . . not yours.

GEORGE

O.K. . . . talk.

NICK

No. *(Pause)* My father-in-law . . . was a man of the Lord, and he was very rich.

GEORGE

What faith?

NICK

He . . . my father-in-law . . . was called by God when he was six, or something, and he started preaching, and he baptized people, and he saved them, and he traveled around a lot, and he became pretty famous . . . not like some of them, but he became pretty famous . . . and when he died he had a lot of money.

GEORGE

God's money.

NICK

No . . . his own.

GEORGE

What happened to God's money?

NICK

He spent God's money . . . and he saved his own. He built hospitals, and he sent off Mercy ships, and he brought the outhouses indoors, and he brought the people outdoors, into the sun, and he built three churches, or whatever they were, and two of them burned down . . . and he ended up pretty rich.

GEORGE *(After considering it)*

Well, I think that's very nice.

NICK

Yes. *(Pause. Giggles a little)* And so, my wife's got some money.

GEORGE

But not God's money.

NICK

No. Her own.

GEORGE

Well, I think that's very nice.

(NICK *giggles a little*)

Martha's got money because Martha's father's second wife . . . not Martha's mother, but after Martha's mother died . . . was a very old lady with warts who was very rich.

NICK

She was a witch.

GEORGE

She was a *good* witch, and she married the white mouse . . .

(NICK *begins to giggle*)

. . . with the tiny red eyes . . . and he must have nibbled her warts, or something like that, because she went up in a puff of smoke almost immediately. POUF!

NICK

POUF!

GEORGE

POUF! And all that was left, aside from some wart medicine, was a big fat will. . . . A peach pie, with some for the township of New Carthage, some for the college, some for Martha's daddy, and just this much for Martha.

NICK (*Quite beside himself*)

Maybe . . . maybe my father-in-law and the witch with the warts should have gotten together, because he was a mouse, too.

GEORGE (*Urging* NICK *on*)

He was?

NICK (*Breaking down*)

Sure . . . he was a church mouse! (*They both laugh a great deal, but it is sad laughter . . . eventually they subside, fall silent*) Your wife never mentioned a stepmother.

GEORGE (*Considers it*)

Well . . . maybe it isn't true.

NICK (*Narrowing his eyes*)

And maybe it is.

GEORGE

Might be . . . might not. Well, I think your story's a lot nicer . . . about your pumped-up little wife, and your father-in-law who was a priest. . . .

NICK

He was not a priest . . . he was a man of God.

GEORGE

Yes.

NICK

And my wife wasn't pumped up . . . she blew up.

GEORGE

Yes, yes.

NICK *(Giggling)*

Get things straight.

GEORGE

I'm sorry . . . I will. I'm sorry.

NICK

O.K.

GEORGE

You realize, of course, that I've been drawing you out on
this stuff, not because I'm interested in your terrible lifehood, but only because you represent a direct and pertinent threat to my lifehood, and I want to get the goods on
you.

NICK *(Still amused)*

Sure . . . sure.

GEORGE

I mean . . . I've warned you . . . you stand warned.

NICK

I stand warned. *(Laughs)* It's you sneaky types worry me
the most, you know. You ineffectual sons of bitches . . .
you're the worst.

GEORGE

Yes . . . we are. Sneaky. An elbow in your steely-blue eye
. . . a knee in your solid gold groin . . . we're the worst.

NICK

Yup.

GEORGE

Well, I'm glad you don't believe me. . . . I know you've got history on your side, and all. . . .

NICK

Unh-unh. *You've* got history on *your* side. . . . I've got biology on mine. History, biology.

GEORGE

I know the difference.

NICK

You don't act it.

GEORGE

No? I thought we'd decided that you'd take over the History Department first, before you took over the whole works. You know . . . a step at a time.

NICK

(Stretching . . . luxuriating . . . playing the game)
Nyaah . . . what I thought I'd do is . . . I'd sort of insinuate myself generally, play around for a while, find all the weak spots, shore 'em up, but with my own name plate on 'em . . . become sort of a fact, and then turn into a . . . a what . . . ?

GEORGE

An inevitability.

NICK

Exactly. . . . An inevitability. You know. . . . Take over a few courses from the older men, start some special groups for myself . . . plow a few pertinent wives. . . .

GEORGE

Now that's it! You can take over all the courses you want to, and get as much of the young elite together in the gymnasium as you like, but until you start plowing per-

tinent wives, you really aren't working. The way to a
man's heart is through his wife's belly, and don't you
forget it.

NICK *(Playing along)*

Yeah. . . . I know.

GEORGE

And the women around here are no better than puntas—
you know, South American ladies of the night. You know
what they do in South America . . . in Rio? The puntas?
Do you know? They hiss . . . like geese. . . . They stand
around in the street and they hiss at you . . . like a bunch
of geese.

NICK

Gangle.

GEORGE

Hm?

NICK

Gangle . . . gangle of geese . . . not bunch . . . gangle.

GEORGE

Well, if you're going to get all cute about it, all ornith-
ological, it's gaggle . . . not gangle, *gaggle*.

NICK

Gaggle? Not gangle?

GEORGE

Yes, gaggle.

NICK *(Crestfallen)*

Oh.

GEORGE

Oh. Yes. . . . Well they stand around on the street and they hiss at you, like a bunch of geese. All the faculty wives, downtown in New Carthage, in front of the A&P, hissing away like a bunch of geese. That's the way to power—plow 'em all!

NICK *(Still playing along)*

I'll bet you're right.

GEORGE

Well, I am.

NICK

And I'll bet your wife's the biggest goose in the gangle, isn't she . . . ? Her father president, and all.

GEORGE

You bet your historical inevitability she is!

NICK

Yessirree. *(Rubs his hands together)* Well now, I'd just better get her off in a corner and mount her like a goddam dog, eh?

GEORGE

Why, you'd certainly better.

NICK

(Looks at GEORGE *a minute, his expression a little sick)* You know, I almost think you're serious.

GEORGE *(Toasting him)*

No, baby . . . *you* almost think you're serious, and it scares the hell out of you.

NICK *(Exploding in disbelief)*

ME!

GEORGE *(Quietly)*

Yes . . . you.

NICK

You're kidding!

GEORGE *(Like a father)*

I wish I were. . . . I'll give you some good advice if you
want me to. . . .

NICK

Good advice! From you? Oh boy! *(Starts to laugh)*

GEORGE

You haven't learned yet. . . . Take it wherever you can
get it. . . . Listen to me, now.

NICK

Come off it!

GEORGE

I'm giving you good advice, now.

NICK

Good God . . . !

GEORGE

There's quicksand here, and you'll be dragged down, just
as. . . .

NICK

Oh boy . . . !

GEORGE

. . before you know it . . . sucked down. . . .
  (NICK laughs derisively)
You disgust me on principle, and you're a smug son of a
bitch personally, but I'm trying to give you a survival kit.
DO YOU HEAR ME?

NICK *(Still laughing)*

I hear you. You come in loud.

GEORGE

ALL RIGHT!

NICK

Hey, Honey.

GEORGE
(Silence. Then quietly)

All right . . . O.K. You want to play it by ear, right? Everything's going to work out anyway, because the time-table's history, right?

NICK

Right . . . right. You just tend to your knitting, grandma. . . . I'll be O.K.

GEORGE *(After a silence)*

I've tried to . . . tried to reach you . . . to. . . .

NICK *(Contemptuously)*

. . . make contact?

GEORGE

Yes.

NICK *(Still)*

. . . communicate?

GEORGE

Yes. Exactly.

NICK

Aw . . . that *is* touching . . . that is . . . downright moving . . . that's what it is. *(With sudden vehemence)* UP YOURS!

GEORGE *(Brief pause)*

Hm?

NICK *(Threatening)*

You heard me!

GEORGE *(At Nick, not to him)*

You take the trouble to construct a civilization . . . to . . . to build a society, based on the principles of . . . of principle . . . you endeavor to make communicable sense out of natural order, morality out of the unnatural disorder of man's mind . . . you make government and art, and realize that they are, must be, both the same . . . you bring things to the saddest of all points . . . to the point where there *is* something to lose . . . then all at once, through all the music, through all the sensible sounds of men building, attempting, comes the *Dies Irae*. And what is it? What does the trumpet sound? Up yours. I suppose there's justice to it, after all the years. . . . Up yours.

NICK
(Brief pause . . . then applauding)

Ha, ha! Bravo! Ha, ha! *(Laughs on)*
(And MARTHA *re-enters, leading* HONEY, *who is wan but smiling bravely)*

HONEY *(Grandly)*

Thank you . . . thank you.

MARTHA

Here we are, a little shaky, but on our feet.

GEORGE

Goodie.

NICK

What? Oh . . . oh! Hi, Honey . . . you better?

HONEY

A little bit, dear. . . . I'd better sit down, though.

NICK

Sure . . . c'mon . . . you sit by me.

HONEY

Thank you, dear.

GEORGE *(Beneath his breath)*

Touching . . . touching.

MARTHA *(To GEORGE)*

Well? Aren't you going to apologize?

GEORGE *(Squinting)*

For what, Martha?

MARTHA

For making the little lady throw up, what else?

GEORGE

I did not make her throw up.

MARTHA

You most certainly did!

GEORGE

I did not!

HONEY *(Papal gesture)*

No, now . . . no.

MARTHA *(To GEORGE)*

Well, who do you think did . . . Sexy over there? You think he made his *own* little wife sick?

GEORGE *(Helpfully)*

Well, you make *me* sick.

MARTHA

THAT'S DIFFERENT!

HONEY

No, now. I . . . I throw up . . . I mean, I get sick . . .
occasionally, all by myself . . . without any reason.

GEORGE

Is that a fact?

NICK

You're . . . you're delicate, Honey.

HONEY *(Proudly)*

I've always done it.

GEORGE

Like Big Ben.

NICK *(A warning)*

Watch itl

HONEY

And the doctors say there's nothing wrong with me . . .
organically. You know?

NICK

Of course there isn't.

HONEY

Why, just before we got married, I developed . . . appendicitis . . . or everybody *thought* it was appendicitis
. . . but it turned out to be . . . it was a . . . *(laughs briefly)*
. . . false alarm.

(GEORGE *and* NICK *exchange glances)*

MARTHA *(To* GEORGE)

Get me a drink.
(GEORGE *moves to the bar)*
George makes everybody sick. . . . When our son was just

a little boy, he used to. . . .

GEORGE

Don't, Martha. . . .

MARTHA

. . . he used to throw up all the time, because of
George. . . .

GEORGE

I said, don't!

MARTHA

It got so bad that whenever George came into the room
he'd start right in retching, and. . . .

GEORGE

. . . the real reason *(Spits out the words)* our son . . .
used to throw up all the time, wife and lover, was nothing more complicated than that he couldn't stand you
fiddling at him all the time, breaking into his bedroom
with your kimono flying, fiddling at him all the time, with
your liquor breath on him, and your hands all over
his. . . .

MARTHA

YEAH? And I suppose that's why he ran away from home
twice in one month, too. *(Now to the guests)* Twice in one
month! Six times in one year!

GEORGE *(Also to the guests)*

Our son ran away from home all the time because Martha
here used to corner him.

MARTHA *(Braying)*

I NEVER CORNERED THE SON OF A BITCH IN MY LIFE!

GEORGE
(Handing MARTHA her drink)

He used to run up to me when I'd get home, and he'd say, "Mama's always coming at me." That's what he'd say.

MARTHA

Liar!

GEORGE *(Shrugging)*

Well, that's the way it was . . . you were always coming at him. I thought it was very embarrassing.

NICK

If you thought it was so embarrassing, what are you talking about it for?

HONEY *(Admonishing)*

Dear . . . !

MARTHA

Yeah! *(To* NICK*)* Thanks, sweetheart.

GEORGE *(To them all)*

I didn't want to talk about him at all . . . I would have been perfectly happy not to discuss the whole subject. . . . I never want to talk about it.

MARTHA

Yes you do.

GEORGE

When we're alone, maybe.

MARTHA

We're alone!

GEORGE

Uh . . . no, Love . . . we've got guests.

MARTHA

(With a covetous look at NICK*)*

We sure have.

HONEY

Could I have a little brandy? I think I'd like a little
brandy.

NICK

Do you think you should?

HONEY

Oh yes . . . yes, dear.

GEORGE
(Moving to the bar again)
Sure! Fill 'er up!

NICK

Honey, I don't think you. . . .

HONEY
(Petulance creeping in)
It will steady me, *dear*. I feel a little unsteady.

GEORGE

Hell, you can't walk steady on half a bottle . . . got to do
it right.

HONEY

Yes. *(To* MARTHA*)* I love brandy . . . I really do.

MARTHA
(Somewhat abstracted)
Good for you.

NICK *(Giving up)*
Well, if you think it's a good idea. . . .

HONEY *(Really testy)*
I know what's best for me, dear.

NICK *(Not even pleasant)*
Yes . . . I'm sure you do.

HONEY
(GEORGE *hands her a brandy*)
Oh, goodie! Thank you. (*To* NICK) Of course I do, dear.

GEORGE (*Pensively*)
I used to drink brandy.

MARTHA (*Privately*)
You used to drink bergin, too.

GEORGE (*Sharp*)
Shut up, Martha!

MARTHA
(*Her hand over her mouth in a little girl gesture*)
Oooooops.

NICK
(*Something having clicked, vaguely*)
Hm?

GEORGE (*Burying it*)
Nothing . . . nothing.

MARTHA (*She, too*)
You two men have it out while we were gone? George
tell you his side of things? He bring you to tears, hunh?

NICK
Well . . . no. . . .

GEORGE
No, what we did, actually, was . . . we sort of danced
around.

MARTHA
Oh, yeah? Cute!

HONEY

Oh, I love dancing.

NICK

He didn't mean that, Honey.

HONEY

Well, I didn't think he did! Two grown men dancing . . .
heavens!

MARTHA

You mean he didn't start in on how he would have
amounted to something if it hadn't been for Daddy? How
his high moral sense wouldn't even let him *try* to better
himself? No?

NICK *(Qualified)*

No. . . .

MARTHA

And he didn't run on about how he tried to publish a goddam book, and Daddy wouldn't let him.

NICK

A book? No.

GEORGE

Please, Martha. . . .

NICK *(Egging her on)*

A book? What book?

GEORGE *(Pleading)*

Please. Just a book.

MARTHA *(Mock incredulity)*

Just a book!

GEORGE

Please, Martha!

MARTHA *(Almost disappointed)*

Well, I guess you didn't get the whole sad story. What's the matter with you, George? You given up?

GEORGE *(Calm . . . serious)*

No . . . no. It's just I've got to figure out some new way to fight you, Martha. Guerilla tactics, maybe . . . internal subversion . . . I don't know. Something.

MARTHA

Well, you figure it out, and you let me know when you do.

GEORGE *(Cheery)*

All right, Love.

HONEY

Why don't we dance? I'd love some dancing.

NICK

Honey. . . .

HONEY

I would! I'd love some dancing.

NICK

Honey. . . .

HONEY

I *want* some! I want some dancing!

GEORGE

All right . . . ! For heaven's sake . . . we'll have some dancing.

HONEY *(All sweetness again)*
(To MARTHA*)* Oh, I'm so glad . . . I just love dancing.
Don't you?

MARTHA
(With a glance at NICK*)*
Yeah . . . yeah, that's not a bad idea.

NICK *(Genuinely nervous)*
Gee.

GEORGE
Gee.

HONEY
I dance like the wind.

MARTHA *(Without comment)*
Yeah?

GEORGE *(Picking a record)*
Martha had her daguerreotype in the paper once . . . oh,
'bout twenty five years ago. . . . Seems she took second
prize in one o' them seven-day dancin' contest things . . .
biceps all bulging, holding up her partner.

MARTHA
Will you put a record on and shut up?

GEORGE
Certainly, Love. *(To all)* How are we going to work this?
Mixed doubles?

MARTHA
Well, you certainly don't think I'm going to dance with
you, do you?

GEORGE *(Considers it)*
Noooooo . . . not with him around . . . that's for sure. And

not with twinkle-toes here, either.

HONEY
I'll dance with anyone. . . . I'll dance by myself.

NICK
Honey. . . .

HONEY
I dance like the wind.

GEORGE
All right, kiddies . . . choose up and hit the sack.
*(Music starts. . . . Second movement, Beethoven's
7th Symphony)*

HONEY
(Up, dancing by herself)
De, de de *da* da, da-da de, da *da*-da de da . . . wonder-
ful . . . !

NICK
Honey. . . .

MARTHA
All right, George . . . cut that out!

HONEY
Dum, de de da da, da-da de, dum de *da* da da. . . .
Wheeeee . . . !

MARTHA
Cut it out, George!

GEORGE
(Pretending not to hear)
What, Martha? What?

NICK
Honey. . . .

MARTHA
(As GEORGE *turns up the volume)*
CUT IT OUT, GEORGE!

GEORGE
WHAT?

MARTHA
(Gets up, moves quickly, threateningly, to GEORGE*)*
All right, you son of a bitch. . . .

GEORGE
(Record off, at once. Quietly)
What did you say, Love?

MARTHA
You son of a. . . .

HONEY
(In an arrested posture)
You stopped! Why did you stop?

NICK
Honey. . . .

HONEY *(To* NICK, *snapping)*
Stop that!

GEORGE
I thought it was fitting, Martha.

MARTHA
Oh you did, hunh?

HONEY
You're always *at* me when I'm having a good time.

NICK *(Trying to remain civil)*

I'm sorry, Honey.

HONEY

Just . . . leave me alone!

GEORGE

Well, why don't *you* choose, Martha? *(Moves away from the phonograph . . . leaves it to* MARTHA*)* Martha's going to run things . . . the little lady's going to lead the band.

HONEY

I like to dance and you don't want me to.

NICK

I like you to dance.

HONEY

Just . . . leave me alone. *(She sits . . . takes a drink)*

GEORGE

Martha's going to put on some rhythm she understands . . . Sacre du Printemps, maybe. *(Moves . . . sits by* HONEY*)* Hi, sexy.

HONEY *(A little giggle-scream)*

Oooooohhhhh!

GEORGE *(Laughs mockingly)*

Ha, ha, ha, ha, ha. Choose it, Martha . . . do your stuff!

MARTHA
(Concentrating on the machine)

You're damn right!

GEORGE *(To* HONEY*)*

You want to dance with me, angel-tits?

NICK

What did you call my wife?

GEORGE *(Derisively)*

Oh boy!

HONEY *(Petulantly)*

No! If I can't do my interpretive dance, I don't want to dance with anyone. I'll just sit here and. . . . *(Shrugs . . . drinks)*

MARTHA

(Record on . . . a jazzy slow pop tune)
O.K. stuff, let's go. *(Grabs* NICK*)*

NICK

Hm? Oh . . . hi.

MARTHA

Hi. *(They dance, close together, slowly)*

HONEY *(Pouting)*

We'll just sit here and watch.

GEORGE

That's *right!*

MARTHA *(To* NICK*)*

Hey, you *are* strong, aren't you?

NICK

Unh-hunh.

MARTHA

I like that.

NICK

Unh-hunh.

HONEY

They're dancing like they've danced before.

GEORGE

It's a familiar dance . . . they both know it. . . .

MARTHA

Don't be shy.

NICK

I'm . . . not. . . .

GEORGE *(To* HONEY)

It's a very old ritual, monkey-nipples . . . old as they come.

HONEY

I . . . I don't know what you mean.
*(NICK and MARTHA move apart now, and dance on
either side of where GEORGE and HONEY are sitting;
they face each other, and while their feet move but
little, their bodies undulate congruently. . . . It is
as if they were pressed together)*

MARTHA

I like the way you move.

NICK

I like the way you move, too.

GEORGE *(To* HONEY)

They like the way they move.

HONEY *(Not entirely with it)*

That's nice.

MARTHA *(To* NICK)

I'm surprised George didn't give you his side of things.

GEORGE *(To* HONEY)

Aren't they cute?

NICK

Well, he didn't.

MARTHA

That surprises me.
(Perhaps MARTHA'S *statements are more or less in time to the music)*

NICK

Does it?

MARTHA

Yeah . . . he usually does . . . when he gets the chance.

NICK

Well, what do you know.

MARTHA

It's really a very sad story.

GEORGE

You have ugly talents, Martha.

NICK

Is it?

MARTHA

It would make you weep.

GEORGE

Hideous gifts.

NICK

Is that so?

GEORGE

Don't encourage her.

MARTHA

Encourage me.

NICK

Go on.
(They may undulate toward each other and then move back)

GEORGE

I warn you . . . don't encourage her.

MARTHA

He warns you . . . don't encourage me.

NICK

I heard him . . . tell me more.

MARTHA
(Consciously making rhymed speech)
Well, Georgie-boy had lots of big ambitions
In spite of something funny in his past. . . .

GEORGE *(Quietly warning)*

Martha. . . .

MARTHA

Which Georgie-boy here turned into a novel. . . .
His first attempt and also his last. . . .
Hey! I rhymed! I rhymed!

GEORGE

I warn you, Martha.

NICK

Yeah . . . you rhymed. Go on, go on.

MARTHA

But daddy took a look at Georgie's novel. . . .

GEORGE

You're looking for a punch in the mouth. . . . You know
that, Martha.

MARTHA

Do tell! . . . and he was very shocked by what he read.

NICK

He was?

MARTHA

Yes . . . he was. . . . A novel all about a naughty boychild. . . .

GEORGE *(Rising)*

I will not tolerate this!

NICK *(Offhand, to* GEORGE*)*

Oh, can it.

MARTHA

. . . ha, ha!
naughty boychild
who . . . uh . . . who killed his mother and his father dead.

GEORGE

STOP IT, MARTHA!

MARTHA

And Daddy said . . . Look here, I will not let you publish
such a thing. . . .

GEORGE
(Rushes to phonograph . . . rips the record off)

That's it! The dancing's over. That's it. Go on now!

NICK

What do you think you're doing, hunh?

HONEY *(Happily)*

Violence! Violence!

MARTHA
(Loud: a pronouncement)

And Daddy said . . . Look here, kid, you don't think for a second I'm going to let you publish this crap, do you? Not on your life, baby . . . not while you're teaching here. . . . You publish that goddam book and you're out . . . on your ass!

GEORGE

DESIST! DESIST!

MARTHA

Ha, ha, ha, HA!

NICK *(Laughing)*

De . . . sist!

HONEY

Oh, violence . . . violence!

MARTHA

Why, the idea! A teacher at a respected, conservative institution like this, in a town like New Carthage, publishing a book like that? If you respect your position here, young man, young . . . whippersnapper, you'll just withdraw that manuscript. . . .

GEORGE

I will not be made mock of!

NICK

He will not be made mock of, for Christ's sake. *(Laughs)*
(HONEY *joins in the laughter, not knowing exactly
why)*

GEORGE

I will not!
            (All three are laughing at him)
(Infuriated) THE GAME IS OVER!

MARTHA *(Pushing on)*

Imagine such a thing! A book about a boy who murders
his mother and kills his father, and pretends it's all an
accident!

HONEY
            (Beside herself with glee)
An accident!

NICK
            (Remembering something related)
Hey . . . wait a minute. . . .

MARTHA *(Her own voice now)*

And you want to know the clincher? You want to know
what big brave Georgie said to Daddy?

GEORGE

NO! NO! NO! NO!

NICK

Wait a minute now. . . .

MARTHA

Georgie said . . . but Daddy . . . I mean . . . ha, ha, ha,
ha . . . but *Sir,* it isn't a *novel* at all. . . . *(Other voice)*
Not a novel? *(Mimicking* GEORGE's *voice)* No, Sir . . . it
isn't a novel at all. . . .

GEORGE *(Advancing on her)*

You will not say this!

NICK *(Sensing the danger)*

Hey.

MARTHA

The hell I won't. Keep away from me, you bastard!
    (Backs off a little ... uses GEORGE's *voice again)*
No, Sir, this isn't a novel at all ... this is the truth ...
this really happened. ... TO ME!

GEORGE *(On her)*

I'LL KILL YOU!
        (Grabs her by the throat. They struggle)

NICK

HEY! *(Comes between them)*

HONEY *(Wildly)*

VIOLENCE! VIOLENCE!
    *(*GEORGE, MARTHA, *and* NICK *struggle ... yells, etc.)*

MARTHA

IT HAPPENED! TO ME! TO ME!

GEORGE

YOU SATANIC BITCH!

NICK

STOP THAT! STOP THAT!

HONEY

VIOLENCE! VIOLENCE!
    (The other three struggle. GEORGE's *hands are on*
MARTHA's *throat.* NICK *grabs him, tears him from*
MARTHA, *throws him on the floor.* GEORGE, *on the*

floor; NICK *over him;* MARTHA *to one side, her hand
on her throat)*

NICK

That's enough now!

HONEY
(Disappointment in her voice)

Oh . . . oh . . . oh. . . .
*(*GEORGE *drags himself into a chair. He is hurt, but
it is more a profound humiliation than a physical
injury)*

GEORGE
(They watch him . . . a pause. . . .)

All right . . . all right . . . very quiet now . . . we will
all be . . . very quiet.

MARTHA
(Softly, with a slow shaking of her head)

Murderer. Mur . . . der . . . er.

NICK *(Softly to* MARTHA*)*

O.K. now . . . that's enough.
*(A brief silence. They all move around a little,
self-consciously, like wrestlers flexing after a fall)*

GEORGE
*(Composure seemingly recovered, but there is a
great nervous intensity)*

Well! That's one game. What shall we do now, hunh?
*(*MARTHA *and* NICK *laugh nervously)*

Oh come on . . . let's think of something else. We've
played Humiliate the Host . . . we've gone through that
one . . . what shall we do now?

NICK

Aw . . . look. . . .

GEORGE

AW LOOK! *(Whines it)* Awww . . . looooook. *(Alert)* I mean, come on! We must know other games, college type types like us . . . that can't be the . . . limit of our vocabulary, can it?

NICK

I think maybe. . . .

GEORGE

Let's see now . . . what else can we do? There are other games. How about . . . how about . . . Hump the Hostess? HUNH?? How about that? How about Hump the Hostess? *(To* NICK*)* You wanna play that one? You wanna play Hump the Hostess? HUNH? HUNH?

NICK *(A little frightened)*

Calm down, now.
            *(*MARTHA *giggles quietly)*

GEORGE

Or is that for later . . . mount her like a goddamn dog?

HONEY

(Wildly toasting everybody)
Hump the Hostess!

NICK *(To* HONEY *. . . sharply)*

Just shut up . . . will you?
            *(*HONEY *does, her glass in mid-air)*

GEORGE

You don't wanna play that now, hunh? You wanna save that game till later? Well, what'll we play now? We gotta play a game.

MARTHA *(Quietly)*

Portrait of a man drowning.

GEORGE
(Affirmatively, but to none of them)
I am not drowning.

HONEY
(To NICK, tearfully indignant)
You told me to shut up!

NICK *(Impatiently)*
I'm sorry.

HONEY *(Between her teeth)*
No you're not.

NICK
(To HONEY, even more impatiently)
I'm sorry.

GEORGE
(Claps his hands together, once, loud)
I've got it! I'll tell you what game we'll play. We're done
with Humiliate the Host . . . this round, anyway . . . we're
done with that . . . and we don't want to play Hump the
Hostess, yet . . . not yet . . . So I know what we'll play.
. . . We'll play a round of Get the Guests. How about
that? How about a little game of Get the Guests?

MARTHA
(Turning away, a little disgusted)
Jesus, George.

GEORGE
Book dropper! Child mentioner!

HONEY
I don't like these games.

NICK

Yeah. . . . I think maybe we've had enough of games, now. . . .

GEORGE

Oh, no . . . oh, no . . . we haven't. We've had only one game. . . . Now we're going to have another. You can't fly on one game.

NICK

I think maybe. . . .

GEORGE *(With great authority)*

SILENCE! *(It is respected)* Now, how are we going to play Get the Guests?

MARTHA

For God's sake, George. . . .

GEORGE

You be quiet!

(MARTHA shrugs)

I wonder. . . . I wonder. *(Puzzles . . . then. . . .)* O.K.! Well . . . Martha . . . in her indiscreet way . . . well, not really indiscreet, because Martha is a naïve, at heart . . . anyway, Martha told you all about my first novel. True or false? Hunh? I mean, true or false that there ever was such a thing. HA! But, Martha told you about it . . . my first novel, my . . . memory book . . . which I'd sort of preferred she hadn't, but hell, that's blood under the bridge. BUT! what she didn't do . . . what Martha didn't tell you about is she didn't tell us all about my *second* novel.

(MARTHA looks at him with puzzled curiosity)

No, you didn't know about that, did you, Martha? About my second novel, true or false. True or false?

MARTHA *(Sincerely)*

No.

GEORGE

No.

*(He starts quietly but as he goes on, his tone be-
comes harsher, his voice louder)*

Well, it's an allegory, really—probably—but it can be read
as straight, cozy prose . . . and it's all about a nice young
couple who come out of the middle west. It's a bucolic
you see. AND, this nice young couple comes out of the
middle west, and he's blond and about thirty, and he's a
scientist, a teacher, a scientist . . . and his mouse is a wifey
little type who gargles brandy all the time . . . and. . . .

NICK

Just a minute here. . . .

GEORGE

. . . and they got to know each other when they was only
teensie little types, and they used to get under the vanity
table and poke around, and. . . .

NICK

I said JUST A MINUTE!

GEORGE

This is my game! You played yours . . . you people. This
is my game!

HONEY *(Dreamy)*

I want to hear the story. I love stories.

MARTHA

George, for heaven's sake. . . .

GEORGE

AND! And Mousie's father was a holy man, see, and he ran
sort of a traveling clip joint, based on Christ and all those
girls, and he took the faithful . . . that's all . . . just took
'em. . . .

HONEY *(Puzzling)*

This is familiar. . . .

NICK *(Voice shaking a little)*

No kidding!

GEORGE

. . . and he died eventually, Mousie's pa, and they pried him open, and all sorts of money fell out. . . . Jesus money, Mary money. . . . LOOT!

HONEY *(Dreamy, puzzling)*

I've heard this story before.

NICK

(With quiet intensity . . . to waken her)

Honey. . . .

GEORGE

But that's in the backwash, in the early part of the book. Anyway, Blondie and his frau out of the plain states came. *(Chuckles)*

MARTHA

Very funny, George. . . .

GEORGE

. . . thank you . . . and settled in a town just like nouveau Carthage here. . . .

NICK *(Threatening)*

I don't think you'd better go on, mister. . . .

GEORGE

Do you not!

NICK *(Less certainly)*

No. I . . . I don't think you'd better.

HONEY

I love familiar stories . . . they're the best.

GEORGE

How right you are. But Blondie was in disguise, really, al
got up as a teacher, 'cause his baggage ticket had bigger
things writ on it . . . H.I. HI! Historical inevitability.

NICK

There's no need for you to go any further, now. . . .

HONEY

(Puzzling to make sense out of what she is hearing)
Let them go on.

GEORGE

We shall. And he had this baggage with him, and par
of this baggage was in the form of his mouse. . . .

NICK

We don't have to listen to this!

HONEY

Why not?

GEORGE

Your bride has a point. And one of the things nobod
could understand about Blondie was his baggage . . . hi
mouse, I mean, here he was, pan-Kansas swimmin
champeen, or something, and he had this mouse, of whom
he was solicitous to a point that faileth human under
standing . . . given that she was sort of a simp, in th
long run. . . .

NICK

This isn't fair of you. . . .

GEORGE

Perhaps not. Like, as I said, his mouse, she tooted brand

immodestly and spent half of her time in the up-chuck. . . .

HONEY *(Focussing)*

I know these people. . . .

GEORGE

Do you! . . . But she was a money baggage amongst other things . . . Godly money ripped from the golden teeth of the unfaithful, a pragmatic extension of the big dream . . . and she was put up with. . . .

HONEY *(Some terror)*

I don't like this story. . . .

NICK *(Surprisingly pleading)*

Please . . . please don't.

MARTHA

Maybe you better stop, George. . . .

GEORGE

. . . and she was put up with. . . . STOP? Ha-ha.

NICK

Please . . . please don't.

GEORGE

Beg, baby.

MARTHA

George. . . .

GEORGE

. . . and . . . oh, we get a flashback here, to How They Got Married.

NICK

NO!

GEORGE *(Triumphant)*

YES!

NICK *(Almost whining)*

Why?

GEORGE

How They Got Married. Well, how they got married is
this. . . . The Mouse got all puffed up one day, and she
went over to Blondie's house, and she stuck out her puff,
and she said . . . look at me.

HONEY *(White . . . on her feet)*

I . . . don't . . . like this.

NICK *(To* GEORGE*)*

Stop it!

GEORGE

Look at me . . . I'm all puffed up. Oh my goodness, said
Blondie. . . .

HONEY *(As from a distance)*

. . . and so they were married. . . .

GEORGE

. . . and so they were married. . . .

HONEY

. . . and then. . . .

GEORGE

. . . and then. . . .

HONEY *(Hysteria)*

WHAT? . . . and then, WHAT?

NICK

NO! No!

GEORGE *(As if to a baby)*

. . . and then the puff went *away* . . . like magic . . . pouf!

NICK *(Almost sick)*

Jesus God. . . .

HONEY

. . . the puff went away. . . .

GEORGE *(Softly)*

. . . pouf.

NICK

Honey . . . I didn't mean to . . . honestly, I didn't mean to. . . .

HONEY

You . . . you told them. . . .

NICK

Honey . . . I didn't mean to. . . .

HONEY
(With outlandish horror)

You . . . told them! You told them! ooooHHHH! Oh, no, no, no! You couldn't have told them . . . oh, noooo!

NICK

Honey, I didn't mean to. . . .

HONEY *(Grabbing at her belly)*

Ohhhhh . . . nooooo.

NICK

Honey . . . baby . . . I'm sorry . . . I didn't mean to. . . .

GEORGE
(Abruptly and with some disgust)
And that's how you play Get the Guests.

HONEY

I'm going to . . . I'm going to be . . . sick. . . .

GEORGE

Naturally!

NICK

Honey. . . .

HONEY (Hysterical)
Leave me alone . . . I'm going . . . to . . . be . . . sick
(She runs out of the room)

MARTHA
(Shaking her head, watching HONEY's retreating form)
God Almighty.

GEORGE (Shrugging)
The patterns of history.

NICK (Quietly shaking)
You shouldn't have done that . . . you shouldn't have done
that at all.

GEORGE (Calmly)
I hate hypocrisy.

NICK

That was cruel . . . and vicious. . . .

GEORGE

. . . she'll get over it. . . .

NICK

... and damaging ... !

GEORGE

... she'll recover. ...

NICK

DAMAGING!! TO ME!!

GEORGE *(With wonder)*

To you!

NICK

TO ME!!

GEORGE

To you!!

NICK

YES!!

GEORGE

Oh beautiful ... beautiful. By God, you gotta have a
swine to show you where the truffles are. *(So calmly)*
Well, you just rearrange your alliances, boy. You just pick
up the pieces where you can ... you just look around and
make the best of things ... you scramble back up on
your feet.

MARTHA *(Quietly, to NICK)*

Go look after your wife.

GEORGE

Yeah ... go pick up the pieces and plan some new strat-
egy.

NICK

(To GEORGE, as he moves toward the hall)

You're going to regret this.

GEORGE

Probably. I regret everything.

NICK

I mean, I'm going to make you regret this.

GEORGE *(Softly)*

No doubt. Acute embarrassment, eh?

NICK

I'll play the charades like you've got 'em set up. . . . I'll play in your language. . . . I'll be what you say I am.

GEORGE

You are already . . . you just don't know it.

NICK *(Shaking within)*

No . . . no. Not really. But I'll *be* it, mister. . . . I'll show you something come to life you'll wish you hadn't set up.

GEORGE

Go clean up the mess.

NICK *(Quietly . . . intensely)*

You just wait, mister.
       (He exits. Pause. GEORGE *smiles at* MARTHA)

MARTHA

Very good, George.

GEORGE

Thank you, Martha.

MARTHA

Really good.

GEORGE

I'm glad you liked it.

MARTHA

I mean. . . . You did a good job . . . you really fixed it.

GEORGE

Unh-hunh.

MARTHA

It's the most . . . life you've shown in a long time.

GEORGE

You bring out the best in me, baby.

MARTHA

Yeah . . . pigmy hunting!

GEORGE

PIGMY!

MARTHA

You're really a bastard.

GEORGE

I? I?

MARTHA

Yeah . . . you.

GEORGE

Baby, if quarterback there is a pigmy, you've certainly changed your style. What are you after now . . . giants?

MARTHA

You make me sick.

GEORGE

It's perfectly all right for you. . . . I mean, you can make your own rules . . . you can go around like a hopped-up

Arab, slashing away at everything in sight, scarring up half the world if you want to. But somebody else try it . . . no sir!

MARTHA

You miserable. . . .

GEORGE *(Mocking)*

Why baby, I did it all for you. I thought you'd like it, sweetheart . . . it's sort of to your taste . . . blood, carnage and all. Why, I thought you'd get all excited . . . sort of heave and pant and come running at me, your melons bobbing.

MARTHA

You've really screwed up, George.

GEORGE *(Spitting it out)*

Oh, for God's sake, Martha!

MARTHA

I mean it . . . you really have.

GEORGE

(Barely contained anger now)

You can sit there in that chair of yours, you can sit there with the gin running out of your mouth, and you can humiliate me, you can tear me apart . . . ALL NIGHT . . . and that's perfectly all right . . . that's O.K. . . .

MARTHA

YOU CAN STAND IT!

GEORGE

I CANNOT STAND IT!

MARTHA

YOU CAN STAND IT!! YOU MARRIED ME FOR IT!!

(A silence)

GEORGE (*Quietly*)

That is a desperately sick lie.

MARTHA

DON'T YOU KNOW IT, EVEN YET?

GEORGE (*Shaking his head*)

Oh . . . Martha.

MARTHA

My arm has gotten tired whipping you.

GEORGE

(*Stares at her in disbelief*)

You're mad.

MARTHA

For twenty-three years!

GEORGE

You're deluded . . . Martha, you're deluded.

MARTHA

IT'S NOT WHAT I'VE WANTED!

GEORGE

I thought at least you were . . . on to yourself. I didn't know. I . . . didn't know.

MARTHA (*Anger taking over*)

I'm on to myself.

GEORGE

(*As if she were some sort of bug*)

No . . . no . . . you're . . . sick.

MARTHA (*Rises—screams*)

I'LL SHOW YOU WHO'S SICK!

GEORGE

All right, Martha . . . you're going too far.

MARTHA *(Screams again)*

I'LL SHOW YOU WHO'S SICK. I'LL SHOW YOU.

GEORGE *(He shakes her)*

Stop it! *(Pushes her back in her chair)* Now, stop it!

MARTHA *(Calmer)*

I'll show you who's sick. *(Calmer)* Boy, you're really having a field day, hunh? Well, I'm going to finish you . . . before I'm through with you. . . .

GEORGE

. . . you and the quarterback . . . you both gonna finish me . . . ?

MARTHA

. . . before I'm through with you you'll wish you'd died in that automobile, you bastard.

GEORGE

(Emphasizing with his forefinger)

And you'll wish you'd never mentioned our son!

MARTHA *(Dripping contempt)*

You. . . .

GEORGE

Now, I said I warned you.

MARTHA

I'm impressed.

GEORGE

I warned you not to go too far.

MARTHA

I'm just beginning.

GEORGE

(Calmly, matter-of-factly)

I'm numbed enough . . . and I don't mean by liquor, though maybe that's been part of the process—a gradual, over-the-years going to sleep of the brain cells—I'm numbed enough, now, to be able to take you when we're alone. I don't listen to you . . . or when I *do* listen to you, I sift everything, I bring everything down to reflex response, so I don't really *hear* you, which is the only way to manage it. But you've taken a new tack, Martha, over the past couple of centuries—or however long it's been I've lived in this house with you—that makes it just too much . . . too much. I don't mind your dirty underthings in public . . . well, I *do* mind, but I've reconciled myself to that . . . but you've moved bag and baggage into your own fantasy world now, and you've started playing variations on your own distortions, and, as a result. . . .

MARTHA

Nuts!

GEORGE

Yes . . . you have.

MARTHA

Nuts!

GEORGE

Well, you can go on like that as long as you want to. And, when you're done. . . .

MARTHA

Have you ever listened to your sentences, George? Have

you ever listened to the way you talk? You're so frig-
ging . . . convoluted . . . that's what you are. You talk like
you were writing one of your stupid papers.

GEORGE

Actually, I'm rather worried about you. About your mind.

MARTHA

Don't you worry about my mind, sweetheart!

GEORGE

I think I'll have you committed.

MARTHA

You WHAT?

GEORGE (*Quietly . . . distinctly*)

I think I'll have you committed.

MARTHA
(*Breaks into long laughter*)

Oh baby, aren't you something!

GEORGE

I've got to find some way to really get at you.

MARTHA

You've got at me, George . . . you don't have to do anything. Twenty-three years of you has been quite enough.

GEORGE

Will you go quietly, then?

MARTHA

You know what's happened, George? You want to know
what's *really happened?* (*Snaps her fingers*) It's snapped,
finally. Not me . . . *it*. The whole arrangement. You can

go along . . . forever, and everything's . . . manageable.
You make all sorts of excuses to yourself . . . *you* know
. . . this is life . . . the hell with it . . . maybe tomorrow
he'll be dead . . . maybe tomorrow *you'll* be dead . . . all
sorts of excuses. But then, one day, one night, something
happens . . . and SNAP! It breaks. And you just don't give
a damn anymore. I've tried with you, baby . . . really, I've
tried.

GEORGE

Come off it, Martha.

MARTHA

I've tried . . . I've really tried.

GEORGE *(With some awe)*

You're a monster . . . you *are*.

MARTHA

I'm loud, and I'm vulgar, and I wear the pants in this
house because somebody's got to, but I am *not* a monster.
I am *not*.

GEORGE

You're a spoiled, self-indulgent, willful, dirty-minded,
liquor-ridden. . . .

MARTHA

SNAP! It went snap. Look, I'm not going to try to get
through to you any more. . . . I'm not going to try. There
was a second back there, maybe, there was a second,
just a second, when I could have gotten through to you,
when maybe we could have cut through all this crap. But
that's past, and now I'm not going to try.

GEORGE

Once a month, Martha! I've gotten used to it . . . once a
month and we get misunderstood Martha, the good-

hearted girl underneath the barnacles, the little Miss
that the touch of kindness'd bring to bloom again. And
I've believed it more times than I want to remember,
because I don't want to think I'm that much of a sucker.
I don't believe you . . . I just don't believe you. There
is no moment . . . there is no moment any more when
we could . . . come together.

MARTHA *(Armed again)*
Well, maybe you're right, baby. You can't come together
with nothing, and you're nothing! SNAP! It went snap tonight at Daddy's party. *(Dripping contempt, but there is
fury and loss under it)* I sat there at Daddy's party, and I
watched you . . . I watched you sitting there, and I
watched the younger men around you, the men who were
going to go somewhere. And I sat there and I watched
you, and *you* weren't *there!* And it snapped! It finally
snapped! And I'm going to howl it out, and I'm not going
to give a damn what I do, and I'm going to make the
damned biggest explosion you ever heard.

GEORGE *(Very pointedly)*
You try it and I'll beat you at your own game.

MARTHA *(Hopefully)*
Is that a threat, George? Hunh?

GEORGE
That's a threat, Martha.

MARTHA *(Fake-spits at him)*
You're going to get it, baby.

GEORGE
Be careful, Martha . . . I'll rip you to pieces.

MARTHA
You aren't man enough . . . you haven't got the guts.

GEORGE

Total war?

MARTHA

Total.

*(Silence. They both seem relieved . . . elated.
NICK re-enters)*

NICK *(Brushing his hands off)*

Well . . . she's . . . resting.

GEORGE

(Quietly amused at NICK's calm, off-hand manner)
Oh?

MARTHA

Yeah? She all right?

NICK

I think so . . . now. I'm . . . terribly sorry. . . .

MARTHA

Forget about it.

GEORGE

Happens all the time around here.

NICK

She'll be all right.

MARTHA

She lying down? You put her upstairs? On a bed?

NICK *(Making himself a drink)*

Well, no, actually. Uh . . . may I? She's . . . in the bathroom . . . on the bathroom floor . . . she's lying there.

GEORGE *(Considers it)*

Well . . . that's not very nice.

NICK

She likes it. She says it's . . . cool.

GEORGE

Still, I don't think. . . .

MARTHA *(Overruling him)*

If she wants to lie on the bathroom floor, let her. *(To NICK, seriously)* Maybe she'd be more comfortable in the tub?

NICK *(He, too, seriously)*

No, she says she likes the floor . . . she took up the mat, and she's lying on the tiles. She . . . she lies on the floor a lot . . . she really does.

MARTHA *(Pause)*

Oh.

NICK

She . . . she gets lots of headaches and things, and she always lies on the floor. *(To GEORGE)* Is there . . . ice?

GEORGE

What?

NICK

Ice. Is there ice?

GEORGE
(As if the word were unfamiliar to him)

Ice?

NICK

Ice. Yes.

MARTHA

Ice.

GEORGE
(As if he suddenly understood)

Ice!

MARTHA

Attaboy.

GEORGE *(Without moving)*

Oh, yes . . . I'll get some.

MARTHA

Well, go. *(Mugging . . . to* NICK*)* Besides, we want to be
alone.

GEORGE
(Moving to take the bucket)

I wouldn't be surprised, Martha . . . I wouldn't be surprised.

MARTHA *(As if insulted)*

Oh, you wouldn't, hunh?

GEORGE

Not a bit, Martha.

MARTHA *(Violent)*

NO?

GEORGE *(He too)*

NO! *(Quietly again)* You'll try anything, Martha.
(Picks up the ice bucket)

NICK *(To cover)*

Actually, she's very . . . frail, and. . . .

GEORGE

. . . slim-hipped.

NICK *(Remembering)*

Yes . . . exactly.

GEORGE
(At the hallway . . . not kindly)
That why you don't have any kids?
(He exits)

NICK
(To GEORGE's retreating form)
Well, I don't know that that's . . . *(Trails off)* . . . if tha
has anything to do with any . . . thing.

MARTHA

Well, if it does, who cares? Hunh?

NICK

Pardon?

(MARTHA blows him a kiss)

NICK
(Still concerned with GEORGE's remark)
I . . . what? . . . I'm sorry.

MARTHA

I said . . . *(Blows him another kiss)*

NICK *(Uncomfortable)*

Oh . . . yes.

MARTHA

Hey . . . hand me a cigarette . . . lover. *(NICK fishes in h*
pocket) That's a good boy. *(He gives her one)* Unh . .
thanks.

*(He lights it for her. As he does, she slips her
hand between his legs, somewhere between the
knee and the crotch, bringing her hand around to
the outside of his leg)*

Ummmmmmmm.

*(He seems uncertain, but does not move. She
smiles, moves her hand a little)*

Now, for being such a good boy, you can give me a kiss.
C'mon.

NICK *(Nervously)*

Look . . . I don't think we should. . . .

MARTHA

C'mon, baby . . . a friendly kiss.

NICK *(Still uncertain)*

Well. . . .

MARTHA

. . . you won't get hurt, little boy. . . .

NICK

. . . not so little. . . .

MARTHA

I'll bet you're not. C'mon. . . .

NICK *(Weakening)*

But what if he should come back in, and . . . or . . . ?

MARTHA

*(All the while her hand is moving up and down
his leg)*

George? Don't worry about him. Besides, who could ob-
ject to a friendly little kiss? It's all in the faculty.

(They both laugh, quietly . . . NICK a little nervously)

We're a close-knit family here . . . Daddy always says so.
. . . Daddy wants us to get to know each other . . . that's
what he had the party for tonight. So c'mon . . . let's get
to know each other a little bit.

NICK

It isn't that I don't want to . . . believe me. . . .

MARTHA

You're a scientist, aren't you? C'mon . . . make an experiment . . . make a little experiment. Experiment on old
Martha.

NICK *(Giving in)*

. . . not very old. . . .

MARTHA

That's right, not very old, but lots of good experience . . .
lots of it.

NICK

I'll . . . I'll bet.

MARTHA
(As they draw slowly closer)
It'll be a nice change for you, too.

NICK

Yes, it would.

MARTHA

And you could go back to your little wife all refreshed.

NICK
(Closer . . . almost whispering)
She wouldn't know the difference.

MARTHA

Well, nobody else's going to know, either.

(They come together. What might have been a joke rapidly becomes serious, with MARTHA *urging it in that direction. There is no frenetic quality, but rather a slow, continually involving intertwining. Perhaps* MARTHA *is still more or less in her chair, and* NICK *is sort of beside and on the chair)*

*(*GEORGE *enters . . . stops . . . watches a moment . . . smiles . . . laughs silently, nods his head, turns, exits, without being noticed)*

*(*NICK, *who has already had his hand on* MARTHA'S *breast, now puts his hand inside her dress)*

MARTHA *(Slowing him down)*

Hey . . . hey. Take it easy, boy. Down, baby. Don't rush it, hunh?

NICK *(His eyes still closed)*

Oh, c'mon, now. . . .

MARTHA *(Pushing him away)*

Unh-unh. Later, baby . . . later.

NICK

I told you . . . I'm a biologist.

MARTHA *(Soothing him)*

I know. I can tell. Later, hunh?

*(*GEORGE *is heard off-stage, singing "Who's afraid of Virginia Woolf?"* MARTHA *and* NICK *go apart,* NICK *wiping his mouth,* MARTHA *checking her clothes. Safely later,* GEORGE *re-enters with the ice bucket)*

GEORGE

. . . of Virginia Woolf,
Virginia Woolf,
Virginia. . . .

... ah! Here we are ... ice for the lamps of China, Man-
churia thrown in. *(To* NICK*)* You better watch those yellow
bastards, my love ... they aren't amused. Why don't you
come on over to our side, and we'll blow the hell out of
'em. Then we can split up the money between us and be
on Easy Street. What d'ya say?

NICK
(Not at all sure what is being talked about)
Well ... sure. Hey! Ice!

GEORGE
(With hideously false enthusiasm)
Right! *(Now to* MARTHA, *purring)* Hello, Martha ... my
dove. ... You look ... radiant.

MARTHA *(Off-hand)*
Thank you.

GEORGE *(Very cheerful)*
Well now, let me see. I've got the ice. ...

MARTHA
... gotten. ...

GEORGE
Got, Martha. Got is perfectly correct ... it's just a little
... archaic, like you.

MARTHA *(Suspicious)*
What are you so cheerful about?

GEORGE *(Ignoring the remark)*
Let's see now ... I've got the ice. Can I make someone a
drink? Martha, can I make you a drink?

MARTHA *(Bravura)*
Yeah, why not?

GEORGE *(Taking her glass)*
Indeed . . . why not? *(Examines the glass)* Martha! You've
been nibbling away at the glass.

MARTHA
I have not!

GEORGE
(To NICK, who is at the bar)
I see you're making your own, which is fine . . . fine. I'll
just hootch up Martha, here, and then we'll be all set.

MARTHA *(Suspicious)*
All set for what?

GEORGE *(Pause . . . considers)*
Why, I don't know. We're having a party, aren't we? *(To
NICK, who has moved from the bar)* I passed your wife in
the hall. I mean, I passed the john and I looked in on her.
Peaceful . . . so peaceful. Sound asleep . . . and she's ac-
tually . . . sucking her thumb.

MARTHA
Awwwwww!

GEORGE
Rolled up like a fetus, sucking away.

NICK *(A little uncomfortably)*
I suppose she's all right.

GEORGE *(Expansively)*
Of course she is! *(Hands MARTHA her drink)* There you
are.

MARTHA *(Still on her guard)*
Thanks.

GEORGE
And now one for me. It's my turn.

MARTHA

Never, baby . . . it's never your turn.

GEORGE *(Too cheerful)*

Oh, now, I wouldn't say that, Martha.

MARTHA

You moving on the principle the worm turns? Well, the worm part's O.K. . . . cause that fits you fine, but the turning part . . . unh-unh! You're in a straight line, buddy-boy, and it doesn't lead anywhere . . . *(A vague afterthought)* . . . except maybe the grave.

GEORGE

(Chuckles, takes his drink)

Well, you just hold that thought, Martha . . . hug it close . . . run your hands over it. Me, I'm going to sit down . . . if you'll excuse me. . . . I'm going to sit down over there and read a book.

(He moves to a chair facing away from the center of the room, but not too far from the front door)

MARTHA

You're gonna do *what?*

GEORGE *(Quietly, distinctly)*

I am going to read a book. Read. Read. Read? You've heard of it? *(Picks up a book)*

MARTHA *(Standing)*

Whaddya mean you're gonna read? What's the matter with you?

GEORGE *(Too calmly)*

There's nothing the matter with me, Martha. . . . I'm going to read a book. That's all.

MARTHA *(Oddly furious)*

We've got company!

GEORGE *(Over-patiently)*

I know, my dear . . . *(Looks at his watch)* . . . but . . . it's after four o'clock, and I always read around this time. Now, you . . . *(Dismisses her with a little wave)* . . . go about your business. . . . I'll sit here very quietly. . . .

MARTHA

You read in the afternoon! You read at four o'clock in the afternoon . . . you don't read at four o'clock in the morning! Nobody reads at four o'clock in the morning!

GEORGE

(Absorbing himself in his book)

Now, now, now.

MARTHA

(Incredulously, to NICK*)*

He's going to read a book. . . . The son of a bitch is going to read a book!

NICK *(Smiling a little)*

So it would seem.

(Moves to MARTHA, *puts his arm around her waist.* GEORGE *cannot see this, of course)*

MARTHA *(Getting an idea)*

Well, we can amuse ourselves, can't we?

NICK

I imagine so.

MARTHA

We're going to amuse ourselves, George.

GEORGE *(Not looking up)*

Unh-hunh. That's nice.

MARTHA

You might not like it.

GEORGE *(Never looking up)*

No, no, now . . . you go right ahead . . . you entertain your guests.

MARTHA

I'm going to entertain myself, too.

GEORGE

Good . . . good.

MARTHA

Ha, ha. You're a riot, George.

GEORGE

Unh-hunh.

MARTHA

Well, I'm a riot, too, George.

GEORGE

Yes you are, Martha.
    (NICK *takes* MARTHA's *hand, pulls her to him.
    They stop for a moment, then kiss, not briefly*)

MARTHA *(After)*

You know what I'm doing, George?

GEORGE

No, Martha . . . what are you doing?

MARTHA

I'm entertaining. I'm entertaining one of the guests. I'm necking with one of the guests.

GEORGE

(Seemingly relaxed and preoccupied, never looking)
Oh, that's nice. Which one?

MARTHA *(Livid)*

Oh, by God you're funny. *(Breaks away from* NICK . . . *moves into* GEORGE's *side-line of vision by herself. Her balance is none too good, and she bumps into or brushes against the door chimes by the door. They chime)*

GEORGE

Someone at the door, Martha.

MARTHA

Never mind that. I said I was necking with one of the guests.

GEORGE

Good . . . good. You go right on.

MARTHA

(Pauses . . . not knowing quite what to do)
Good?

GEORGE

Yes, good . . . good for you.

MARTHA

(Her eyes narrowing, her voice becoming hard)
Oh, I see what you're up to, you lousy little. . . .

GEORGE

I'm up to page a hundred and. . . .

MARTHA

Cut it! Just cut it out! *(She hits against the door chimes again; they chime)* Goddam bongs.

GEORGE

They're chimes, Martha. Why don't you go back to your necking and stop bothering me? I want to read.

MARTHA

Why, you miserable. . . . I'll show *you*.

GEORGE

(Swings around to face her . . . says, with great loathing)
No . . . show him, Martha . . . he hasn't seen it. *Maybe*
he hasn't seen it. *(Turns to* NICK*)* You haven't seen it yet,
have you?

NICK

(Turning away, a look of disgust on his face)
I . . . I have no respect for you.

GEORGE

And none for yourself, either. . . . *(Indicating* MARTHA*)*
I don't know what the younger generation's coming to.

NICK

You don't . . . you don't even. . . .

GEORGE

Care? You're quite right. . . . I couldn't care less. So, you
just take this bag of laundry here, throw her over your
shoulder, and. . . .

NICK

You're disgusting.

GEORGE *(Incredulous)*

Because *you're* going to hump Martha, *I'm* disgusting?
(He breaks down in ridiculing laughter)

MARTHA *(To* GEORGE*)*

You Mother! *(To* NICK*)* Go wait for me, hunh? Go wait
for me in the kitchen. *(But* NICK *does not move.* MARTHA
goes to him, puts her arms around him) C'mon, baby . . .
please. Wait for me . . . in the kitchen . . . be a good
baby.
    *(*NICK *takes her kiss, glares at* GEORGE *. . . who
    has turned his back again . . . and exits)*

exhibitionistic

(MARTHA *swings around to* GEORGE)
Now you listen to me. . . .

GEORGE

I'd rather read, Martha, if you don't mind. . . .

MARTHA

*(Her anger has her close to tears, her frustration
to fury)*
Well, I do mind. Now, you pay attention to me! You come
off this kick you're on, or I swear to God I'll do it. I swear
to God I'll follow that guy into the kitchen, and then I'll
take him upstairs, and. . . .

GEORGE

(Swinging around to her again . . . loud . . . loathing)
SO WHAT, MARTHA?

MARTHA

*(Considers him for a moment . . . then, nodding
her head, backing off slowly)*
O.K. . . . O.K. . . . You asked for it . . . and you're going
to get it.

GEORGE *(Softly, sadly)*

Lord, Martha, if you want the boy that much . . . have him
. . . but do it honestly, will you? Don't cover it over with
all this . . . all this . . . footwork.

MARTHA *(Hopeless)*

I'll make you sorry you made me want to marry you. *(At
the hallway)* I'll make you regret the day you ever decided
to come to this college. I'll make you sorry you ever let
yourself down.

(She exits)
(Silence. GEORGE *sits still, staring straight ahead.
Listening . . . but there is no sound. Outwardly*

calm, he returns to his book, reads a moment,
then looks up . . . considers. . . .)

GEORGE

"And the west, encumbered by crippling alliances, and
burdened with a morality too rigid to accommodate itself
to the swing of events, must . . . eventually . . . fall."
(He laughs, briefly, ruefully . . . rises, with the
book in his hand. He stands still . . . then, quick-
ly, he gathers all the fury he has been containing
within himself . . . he shakes . . . he looks at the
book in his hand and, with a cry that is part
growl, part howl, he hurls it at the chimes. They
crash against one another, ringing wildly. A brief
pause, then HONEY *enters)*

HONEY

(The worse for wear, half asleep, still sick, weak,
still staggering a little . . . vaguely, in something
of a dream world)
Bells. Ringing. I've been hearing bells.

GEORGE

Jesus!

HONEY

I couldn't sleep . . . for the bells. Ding-ding, bong . . . it
woke me up. What time is it?

GEORGE
(Quietly beside himself)
Don't bother me.

HONEY
(Confused and frightened)
I was asleep, and the bells started . . . they BOOMED! Poe-
bells . . . they were Poe-bells . . . Bing-bing-bong-BOOM!

GEORGE

BOOM!

HONEY

I was asleep, and I was dreaming of . . . something . . .
and I heard the sounds coming, and I didn't know what it
was.

GEORGE *(Never quite to her)*

It was the sound of bodies. . . .

HONEY

And I didn't want to wake up, but the sound kept coming. . . .

GEORGE

. . . go back to sleep. . . .

HONEY

. . . and it FRIGHTENED ME!

GEORGE

(Quietly . . . to MARTHA, *as if she were in the room)*

I'm going to get you . . . Martha.

HONEY

And it was so . . . cold. The wind was . . . the wind was
so cold! And I was lying somewhere, and the covers kept
slipping away from me, and I didn't want them to. . . .

GEORGE

Somehow, Martha.

HONEY

. . . and there was someone there . . . !

GEORGE

There was no one there.

HONEY *(Frightened)*
And I didn't want someone there. . . . I was . . . naked . . . !

GEORGE
You don't know what's going on, do you?

HONEY *(Still with her dream)*
I DON'T WANT ANY . . . NO . . . !

GEORGE
You don't know what's been going on around here while
you been having your snoozette, do you.

HONEY
NO! . . . I DON'T WANT ANY . . . I DON'T WANT THEM. . . .
GO 'WAY. . . . *(Begins to cry)* I DON'T WANT . . . ANY . . .
CHILDREN. . . . I . . . don't . . . want . . . any . . . chil-
dren. I'm afraid! I don't want to be hurt. . . . PLEASE!

GEORGE
(Nodding his head . . . speaks with compassion)
I should have known.

HONEY
(Snapping awake from her reverie)
What! What?

GEORGE
I should have known . . . the whole business . . . the headaches . . . the whining . . . the. . . .

HONEY *(Terrified)*
What are you talking about?

GEORGE *(Ugly again)*
Does *he* know that? Does that . . . stud you're married to

know about that, hunh?

HONEY
About what? Stay away from me!

GEORGE
Don't worry, baby . . . I wouldn't. . . . Oh, my God, that
would be a joke, wouldn't it! But don't worry, baby. HEY!
How you do it? Hunh? How do you make your secret
little murders stud-boy doesn't know about, hunh? Pills?
PILLS? You got a secret supply of pills? Or what? Apple
jelly? WILL POWER?

HONEY
I feel sick.

GEORGE
You going to throw up again? You going to lie down on
the cold tiles, your knees pulled up under your chin, your
thumb stuck in your mouth . . . ?

HONEY *(Panicked)*
Where is he?

GEORGE
Where's who? There's nobody here, baby.

HONEY
I want my husband! I want a drink!

GEORGE
Well, you just crawl over to the bar and make yourself
one.
> *(From off-stage comes the sound of* MARTHA's
> *laughter and the crashing of dishes)*

(Yelling) That's right! Go at it!

HONEY
I want . . . something. . . .

GEORGE

You know what's going on in there, little Miss? Hunh?
You hear all that? You know what's going on in there?

HONEY

I don't want to know anything!

GEORGE

There are a couple of people in there. . . .
          (MARTHA's *laughter again*)
. . . they are in there, in the kitchen. . . . Right there, with
the onion skins and the coffee grounds . . . sort of . . .
sort of a . . . sort of a dry run for the wave of the future.

HONEY *(Beside herself)*

I . . . don't . . . understand . . . you. . . .

GEORGE *(A hideous elation)*

It's very simple. . . . When people can't abide things as
they are, when they can't abide the present, they do one
of two things . . . either they . . . either they turn to a con-
templation of the past, as I have done, or they set about to
. . . alter the future. And when you want to change something . . . you BANG! BANG! BANG! BANG!

HONEY

Stop it!

GEORGE

And you, you simpering bitch . . . you don't want *children?*

HONEY

You leave me . . . alone. Who . . . WHO RANG?

GEORGE

What?

HONEY

What were the bells? Who rang?

GEORGE

You don't want to know, do you? You don't want to listen to it, hunh?

HONEY *(Shivering)*

I don't want to listen to you. . . . I want to know who rang.

GEORGE

Your husband is . . . and you want to know who *rang?*

HONEY

Who rang? Someone rang!

GEORGE

(His jaw drops open . . . he is whirling with an idea)
. . . Someone. . . .

HONEY

RANG!

GEORGE

. . . someone . . . rang . . . yes . . . yessss. . . .

HONEY

The . . . bells . . . rang. . . .

GEORGE

(His mind racing ahead)
The bells rang . . . and it was someone. . . .

HONEY

Somebody. . . .

GEORGE

(He is home, now)

... somebody rang ... it was somebody ... with ...
I'VE GOT IT! I'VE GOT IT, MARTHA ... ! Somebody with a
message ... and the message was ... our son ... OUR
SON! *(Almost whispered)* It was a message ... the bells
rang and it was a message, and it was about ... our son
... and the message ... was ... and the message was
... our ... son ... is ... DEAD!

HONEY *(Almost sick)*

Oh ... no.

GEORGE
(Cementing it in his mind)
Our son is ... dead. ... And ... Martha doesn't know.
... I haven't told ... Martha.

HONEY

No ... no ... no.

GEORGE *(Slowly, deliberately)*
Our son is dead, and Martha doesn't know.

HONEY

Oh. God in heaven ... no.

GEORGE
(To HONEY ... slowly, deliberately, dispassionately)
And you're not going to tell her.

HONEY *(In tears)*

Your son is dead.

GEORGE

I'll tell her myself ... in good time. I'll tell her myself.

HONEY *(So faintly)*

I'm going to be sick.

GEORGE

(Turning away from her . . . he, too, softly)

Are you? That's nice.

   (MARTHA's laugh is heard again)

Oh, listen to that.

HONEY

I'm going to die.

GEORGE

(Quite by himself now)

Good . . . good . . . you go right ahead.

   (Very softly, so MARTHA could not possibly hear)

Martha? Martha? I have some . . . terrible news for you.

   (There is a strange half-smile on his lips)

It's about our . . . son. He's dead. Can you hear me, Martha? Our boy is dead.

   (He begins to laugh, very softly . . . it is mixed with crying)

CURTAIN

ACT THREE

THE EXORCISM

(MARTHA *enters, talking to herself*)

MARTHA

Hey, hey. . . . Where is everybody . . . ? *(It is evident she is not bothered)* So? Drop me; pluck me like a goddamn . . . whatever-it-is . . . creeping vine, and throw me over your shoulder like an old shoe . . . George? *(Looks about her)* George? *(Silence)* George! What are you doing: Hiding, or something? *(Silence)* GEORGE!! *(Silence)* Oh, fa Chri. . . . *(Goes to the bar, makes herself a drink and amuses herself with the following performance)* Deserted! Abandon-ed! Left out in the cold like an old pussycat. HA! Can I get you a drink, Martha? Why, thank you, George; that's very kind of you. No, Martha, no; why I'd do anything for you. Would you, George? Why, I'd do anything for you, too. Would you, Martha? Why, certainly, George. Martha, I've misjudged you. And I've misjudged you, too, George. WHERE IS EVERYBODY!!! Hump the Hostess! *(Laughs greatly at this, falls into a chair; calms down, looks defeated, says, softly)* Fat chance. *(Even softer)* Fat chance. *(Baby-talk now)* Daddy? Daddy? Martha is abandon-ed. Left to her own vices at . . . *(Peers at a clock)* . . . something o'clock in the old A.M. Daddy White-Mouse; do you really have red eyes? Do you? Let me see. Ohhhhh! You do! You do! Daddy, you have red eyes . . . because you cry all the time, don't you, Daddy. Yes; you do. You cry alllll the time. I'LL GIVE ALL YOU BASTARDS FIVE TO COME OUT FROM WHERE YOU'RE HIDING!! *(Pause)* I cry all the time too, Daddy. I cry alllll the time; but deep inside, so no one can see me. I cry all the time. And Georgie cries all the time, too. We both cry all the time, and then, what we do, we cry, and we take our tears, and we put 'em in the ice box, in the goddamn ice trays *(Begins to laugh)* until they're all frozen *(Laughs even more)* and then . . . we put them . . . in our . . . drinks. *(More laughter, which is something else, too. After sobering silence)* Up the drain, down the spout, dead, gone and forgotten. . . . Up the spout, not down the spout; *Up* the spout: THE POKER NIGHT. Up the spout. . . . *(Sadly)* I've got windshield wipers on my eyes, because I married you . . . baby! . . . Martha, you'll be a song-writer yet. *(Jiggles the ice in her glass)* CLINK! *(Does it again)* CLINK! *(Giggles, repeats it several times)* CLINK! . . . CLINK! . . . CLINK! . . . CLINK!

(NICK *enters while* MARTHA *is clinking; he stands in the hall entrance and watches her; finally he comes in)*

NICK

My God, you've gone crazy too.

MARTHA

Clink?

NICK

I said, you've gone crazy too.

MARTHA *(Considers it)*

Probably . . . probably.

NICK

You've all gone crazy: I come downstairs, and what happens. . . .

MARTHA

What happens?

NICK

. . . my wife's gone into the can with a liquor bottle, and

she winks at me . . . winks at me! . . .

MARTHA (*Sadly*)

She's never wunk at you; what a shame. . . .

NICK

She is lying down on the floor again, the tiles, all curled up, and she starts peeling the label off the liquor bottle, the brandy bottle. . . .

MARTHA

. . . we'll never get the deposit back that way. . . .

NICK

. . . and I ask her what she's doing, and she goes: shhhhhh! nobody knows I'm here; and I come back in here, and you're sitting there going Clink! for God's sake. Clink!

MARTHA

CLINK!

NICK

You've all gone crazy.

MARTHA

Yes. Sad but true.

NICK

Where is your husband?

MARTHA

He is vanish-ed. Pouf!

NICK

You're all crazy: nuts.

MARTHA (*Affects a brogue*)

Awww, 'tis the refuge we take when the unreality of the

world weighs too heavy on our tiny heads. *(Normal voice again)* Relax; sink into it; you're no better than anybody else.

NICK *(Wearily)*

I think I am.

MARTHA
(Her glass to her mouth)

You're certainly a flop in some departments.

NICK *(Wincing)*

I beg your pardon . . . ?

MARTHA *(Unnecessarily loud)*

I said, you're certainly a flop in some. . . .

NICK *(He, too, too loud)*

I'm sorry you're disappointed.

MARTHA *(Braying)*

I didn't say I was disappointed! Stupid!

NICK

You should try me some time when we haven't been drinking for ten hours, and maybe. . . .

MARTHA *(Still braying)*

I wasn't talking about your potential; I was talking about your goddamn performance.

NICK *(Softly)*

Oh.

MARTHA *(She softer, too)*

Your potential's fine. It's dandy. *(Wiggles her eyebrows)* Absolutely dandy. I haven't seen such a dandy potential in a long time. Oh, but baby, you sure are a flop.

> NICK *(Snapping it out)*

Everybody's a flop to you! Your husband's a flop, *I'm* a flop. . . .

> MARTHA *(Dismissing him)*

You're all flops. I am the Earth Mother, and you're all flops. *(More or less to herself)* I disgust me. I pass my life in crummy, totally pointless infidelities . . . *(Laughs ruefully) would*-be infidelities. Hump the Hostess? That's a laugh. A bunch of boozed-up . . . impotent lunk-heads. Martha makes goo-goo eyes, and the lunk-heads grin, and roll their beautiful, beautiful eyes back, and grin some more, and Martha licks her chops, and the lunk-heads slap over to the bar to pick up a little courage, *and* they pick up a little courage, and they bounce back over to old Martha, who does a little dance for them, which heats them all up . . . mentally . . . and so they slap over to the bar again, and pick up a little more courage, and their wives and sweethearts stick their noses up in the air . . . right through the ceiling, sometimes . . . which sends the lunk-heads back to the soda fountain again where they fuel up some more, while Martha-poo sits there with her dress up over her head . . . suffocating—you don't know how *stuffy* it is with your dress up over your head —suffocating! waiting for the lunk-heads; so, *finally* they get their courage up . . . but that's all, baby! Oh my, there is sometimes some very nice potential, but, oh my! My, my, my. *(Brightly)* But that's how it is in a civilized society. *(To herself again)* All the gorgeous lunk-heads. Poor babies. *(To NICK, now; earnestly)* There is only one man in my life who has ever . . . made me happy. Do you know that? One!

NICK

The . . . the what-do-you-call-it? . . . uh . . . the lawn mower, or something?

MARTHA

No; I'd forgotten him. But when I think about him and me it's almost like being a voyeur. Hunh. No; I didn't mean him; I meant George, of course. *(No response from* NICK*)* Uh . . . George; my husband.

NICK *(Disbelieving)*

You're kidding.

MARTHA

Am I?

NICK

You must be. Him?

MARTHA

Him.

NICK *(As if in on a joke)*

Sure; sure.

MARTHA

You don't believe it.

NICK *(Mocking)*

Why, of course I do.

MARTHA

You always deal in appearances?

NICK *(Derisively)*

Oh, for God's sake. . . .

MARTHA

. . . George who is out somewhere there in the dark. . . . George who is good to me, and whom I revile; who understands me, and whom I push off; who can make me laugh, and I choke it back in my throat; who can hold me, at night, so that it's warm, and whom I will bite so there's blood; who keeps learning the games we play as quickly as I can change the rules; who can make me happy and I do not wish to be happy, and yes I do wish to be happy. George and Martha: sad, sad, sad.

NICK
(Echoing, still not believing)

Sad.

MARTHA

. . . whom I will not forgive for having come to rest; for having seen me and having said: yes; this will do; who has made the hideous, the hurting, the insulting mistake of loving me and must be punished for it. George and Martha: sad, sad, sad.

NICK *(Puzzled)*

Sad.

MARTHA

. . . who tolerates, which is intolerable; who is kind, which is cruel; who understands, which is beyond comprehension. . . .

NICK

George and Martha: sad, sad, sad.

MARTHA

Some day . . . hah! some *night* . . . some stupid, liquor-ridden night . . . I will go too far . . . and I'll either break the man's back . . . or push him off for good . . . which is what I deserve.

NICK

I don't think he's got a vertebra intact.

MARTHA *(Laughing at him)*

You don't, huh? You don't think so. Oh, little boy, you
got yourself hunched over that microphone of yours. . . .

NICK

Microscope. . . .

MARTHA

. . . yes . . . and you don't see anything, do you? You see
everything but the goddamn mind; you see all the little
specks and crap, but you don't see what goes on, do you?

NICK

I know when a man's had his back broken; I can see that.

MARTHA

Can you!

NICK

You're damn right.

MARTHA

Oh . . . you know so little. And you're going to take over
the world, hunh?

NICK

All right, now. . . .

MARTHA

You think a man's got his back broken 'cause he makes
like a clown and walks bent, hunh? Is that *really* all you
know?

NICK

I said, all *right!*

MARTHA

Ohhhh! The stallion's mad, hunh. The gelding's all upset.
Ha, ha, ha, HA!

NICK *(Softly; wounded)*

You . . . you swing wild, don't you.

MARTHA *(Triumphant)*

HAH!

NICK

Just . . . anywhere.

MARTHA

HAH! I'm a Gatling gun. Hahahahahahahahaha!

NICK *(In wonder)*

Aimless . . . butchery. Pointless.

MARTHA

Aw! You poor little bastard.

NICK

Hit out at everything.
(The door chimes chime)

MARTHA

Go answer the door.

NICK *(Amazed)*

What did you say?

MARTHA

I said, go answer the door. What are you, deaf?

NICK
(Trying to get it straight)

You . . . want me . . . to go answer the door?

MARTHA

That's right, lunk-head; answer the door. There must be
something you can do well; or, are you too drunk to do
that, too? Can't you get the latch up, either?

NICK

Look, there's no need. . . .
(Door chimes again)

MARTHA *(Shouting)*

Answer it! *(Softer)* You can be houseboy around here for
a while. You can start off being houseboy right now.

NICK

Look, lady, I'm no flunky to you.

MARTHA *(Cheerfully)*

Sure you are! You're ambitious, aren't you, boy? You
didn't chase me around the kitchen and up the goddamn
stairs out of mad, driven passion, did you now? You were
thinking a little bit about your career, weren't you? Well,
you can just houseboy your way up the ladder for a while.

NICK

There's no limit to you, is there?
(Door chimes again)

MARTHA *(Calmly, surely)*

No, baby; none. Go answer the door. (NICK *hesitates)*
Look, boy; once you stick your nose in it, you're not going
to pull out just whenever you feel like it. You're in for a
while. Now, git!

NICK

Aimless . . . wanton . . . pointless. . . .

MARTHA

Now, now, now; just do what you're told; show old Martha there's something you *can* do. Hunh? Atta boy.

NICK

*(Considers, gives in, moves toward the door. Chimes
again)*

I'm coming, for Christ's sake!

> MARTHA *(Claps her hands)*

Ha HA! Wonderful; marvelous. *(Sings)* "Just a gigolo, everywhere I go, people always say. . . ."

> NICK

STOP THAT!

> MARTHA *(Giggles)*

Sorry, baby; go on now; open the little door.

> NICK *(With great rue)*

Christ.

> *(He flings open the door, and a hand thrusts into the opening a great bunch of snapdragons; they stay there for a moment. NICK strains his eyes to see who is behind them)*

> MARTHA

Oh, how lovely!

> GEORGE

> *(Appearing in the doorway, the snapdragons covering his face; speaks in a hideously cracked falsetto)*

Flores; flores para los muertos. Flores.

> MARTHA

Ha, ha, ha HA!

> GEORGE

> *(A step into the room; lowers the flowers; sees NICK; his face becomes gleeful; he opens his arms)*

Sonny! You've come home for your birthday! At last!

> NICK *(Backing off)*

Stay away from me.

MARTHA

Ha, ha, ha, HA! That's the houseboy, for God's sake.

GEORGE

Really? That's not our own little sonny-Jim? Our own little all-American something-or-other?

MARTHA *(Giggling)*

Well, I certainly hope not; he's been acting awful funny, if he is.

GEORGE *(Almost manic)*

Ohhhh! I'll bet! Chippie-chippie-chippie, hunh? *(Affecting embarrassment)* I . . . I brungya dese flowers, Mart'a, 'cause I . . . wull, 'cause you'se . . . awwwwww hell. Gee.

MARTHA

Pansies! Rosemary! Violence! My wedding bouquet!

NICK *(Starting to move away)*

Well, if you two kids don't mind, I think I'll just. . . .

MARTHA

Ach! You just stay where you are. Make my hubby a drink.

NICK

I don't think I will.

GEORGE

No, Martha, no; that would be too much; he's your house-boy, baby, not mine.

NICK

I'm nobody's houseboy. . . .

GEORGE *and* MARTHA

. . . Now! *(Sing)* I'm nobody's houseboy now. . . . *(Both laugh)*

NICK

Vicious. . . .

GEORGE *(Finishing it for him)*

. . . children. Hunh? That right? Vicious children, with their oh-so-sad games, hopscotching their way through life, etcetera, etcetera. Is that it?

NICK

Something like it.

GEORGE

Screw, baby.

MARTHA

Him can't. Him too fulla booze.

GEORGE

Weally? *(Handing the snapdragons to* NICK*)* Here; dump these in some gin. (NICK *takes them, looks at them, drops them on the floor at his feet)*

MARTHA *(Sham dismay)*

Awwwwwww.

GEORGE

What a terrible thing to do . . . to Martha's snapdragons.

MARTHA

Is that what they are?

GEORGE

. . . up. And here I went out into the moonlight to pick 'em for Martha tonight, and for our sonny-boy tomorrow, for his birfday.

MARTHA
(Passing on information)

There is no moon now. I saw it go down from the bed-room.

GEORGE *(Feigned glee)*

From the bedroom! *(Normal tone)* Well, there was a moon.

MARTHA
(Too patient; laughing a little)

There couldn't have been a moon.

GEORGE

Well, there was. There is.

MARTHA

There is no moon; the moon went down.

GEORGE

There is a moon; the moon is up.

MARTHA
(Straining to keep civil)

I'm afraid you're mistaken.

GEORGE *(Too cheerful)*

No; no.

MARTHA *(Between her teeth)*

There is no goddamn moon.

GEORGE

My dear Martha . . . I did not pick snapdragons in the stony dark. I did not go stumbling around Daddy's green-house in the pitch.

MARTHA

Yes . . . you did. You would.

GEORGE

Martha, I do not pick flowers in the blink. I have neve

robbed a hothouse without there is a light from heaven.

MARTHA *(With finality)*
There is no moon; the moon went down.

GEORGE *(With great logic)*
That may very well be, Chastity; the moon may very well
have gone down . . . but it came back up.

MARTHA
The moon does *not* come back up; when the moon has
gone down it stays down.

GEORGE *(Getting a little ugly)*
You don't know anything. IF the moon went down, then
it came back up.

MARTHA
BULL!

GEORGE
Ignorance! Such . . . ignorance.

MARTHA
Watch who you're calling ignorant!

GEORGE
Once . . . once, when I was sailing past Majorca, drinking
on deck with a correspondent who was talking about Roo-
sevelt, the moon went down, thought about it for a little
. . . considered it, you know what I mean? . . . and then,
POP, came up again. Just like that.

MARTHA
That is not true! That is such a lie!

GEORGE
You must not call everything a lie, Martha. *(To* NICK)
Must she?

NICK

Hell, I don't know when you people are lying, or what.

MARTHA

You're damned right!

GEORGE

You're not supposed to.

MARTHA

Right!

GEORGE

At any rate, I was sailing past Majorca. . . .

MARTHA

You never sailed past Majorca. . . .

GEORGE

Martha. . . .

MARTHA

You were never in the goddamn Mediterranean at all . . .
ever. . . .

GEORGE

I certainly was! My Mommy and Daddy took me there as
a college graduation present.

MARTHA

Nuts!

NICK

Was this after you killed them?
     (GEORGE *and* MARTHA *swing around and look at
     him; there is a brief, ugly pause*)

GEORGE *(Defiantly)*

Maybe.

MARTHA

Yeah; maybe not, too.

NICK

Jesus!

(GEORGE *swoops down, picks up the bunch of snapdragons, shakes them like a feather duster in* NICK's *face, and moves away a little*)

GEORGE

HAH!

NICK

Damn you.

GEORGE (*To* NICK)

Truth and illusion. Who knows the difference, eh, toots? Eh?

MARTHA

You were never in the Mediterranean . . . truth or illusion . . . either way.

GEORGE

If I wasn't in the Mediterranean, how did I get to the Aegean? Hunh?

MARTHA

OVERLAND!

NICK

Yeah!

GEORGE

Don't you side with her, houseboy.

NICK

I am not a houseboy.

GEORGE

Look! I know the game! You don't make it in the sack,
you're a houseboy.

NICK

I AM NOT A HOUSEBOY!

GEORGE

No? Well then, you must have made it in the sack. Yes?
(*He is breathing a little heavy; behaving a little manic*)
Yes? Someone's lying around here; somebody isn't playing the game straight. Yes? Come on; come on; who's lying? Martha? Come on!

NICK

(*After a pause; to* MARTHA, *quietly with intense pleading*)
Tell him I'm not a houseboy.

MARTHA

(*After a pause, quietly, lowering her head*)
No; you're not a houseboy.

GEORGE (*With great, sad relief*)

So be it.

MARTHA (*Pleading*)

Truth and illusion, George; you don't know the difference.

GEORGE

No; but we must carry on as though we did.

MARTHA

Amen.

GEORGE

(*Flourishing the flowers*)
SNAP WENT THE DRAGONS!! (NICK *and* MARTHA *laugh
weakly*)

Hunh? Here we go round the mulberry bush, hunh?

NICK *(Tenderly, to* MARTHA*)*

Thank you.

MARTHA

Skip it.

GEORGE *(Loud)*

I said, here we go round the mulberry bush!

MARTHA *(Impatiently)*

Yeah, yeah; we know; snap go the dragons.

GEORGE

*(Taking a snapdragon, throwing it, spear-like,
stemfirst at* MARTHA*)*

SNAP!

MARTHA

Don't, George.

GEORGE *(Throws another)*

SNAP!

NICK

Don't do that.

GEORGE

Shut up, stud.

NICK

I'm not a stud!

GEORGE *(Throws one at* NICK*)*

SNAP! Then you're a houseboy. Which is it? Which are
you? Hunh? Make up your mind. Either way.... *(Throws*

another at him) SNAP! *you disgust me.*

MARTHA

Does it matter to you, George!?

GEORGE *(Throws one at her)*

SNAP! No, actually, it doesn't. Either way . . . I've had it.

MARTHA

Stop throwing those goddamn things at me!

GEORGE

Either way. *(Throws another at her)* SNAP!

NICK *(To* MARTHA)

Do you want me to . . . do something to him?

MARTHA

You leave him alone!

GEORGE

If you're a houseboy, baby, you can pick up after me; if you're a stud, you can go protect your plow. Either way. Either way. . . . Everything.

NICK

Oh for God's. . . .

MARTHA *(A little afraid)*

Truth or illusion, George. Doesn't it matter to you . . . at all?

GEORGE

(Without throwing anything)

SNAP! *(Silence)* You got your answer, baby?

MARTHA *(Sadly)*

Got it.

GEORGE

You just gird your blue-veined loins, girl. *(Sees* NICK *moving toward the hall)* Now; we got one more game to play. And it's called Bringing Up Baby.

NICK
(More-or-less under his breath)
Oh, for Lord's sake. . . .

MARTHA

George. . . .

GEORGE

I don't want any fuss. *(To* NICK*)* You don't want any scandal around here, do you, big boy? You don't want to wreck things, do you? Hunh? You want to keep to your timetable, don't you? Then sit! *(*NICK *sits) (To* MARTHA*)* And you, pretty Miss, you like fun and games, don't you? You're a sport from way back, aren't you?

MARTHA *(Quietly, giving in)*
All right, George; all right.

GEORGE
(Seeing them both cowed; purrs)
Goooooooood; gooooood. *(Looks about him)* But, we're not all here. *(Snaps his fingers a couple of times at* NICK*)* You; you . . . uh . . . you; your little wifelet isn't here.

NICK

Look; she's had a rough night, now; she's in the can, and she's. . . .

GEORGE

Well, we can't play without everyone here. Now that's a fact. We gotta have your little wife. *(Hog-calls toward the hall)* sooowwwwiiieee!! sooowwwwiiieee!!

NICK
(As MARTHA *giggles nervously)*
Cut that!

GEORGE
(Swinging around, facing him)
Then get your butt out of that chair and bring the little
dip back in here. *(As* NICK *does not move)* Now be a good
puppy. Fetch, good puppy, go fetch.
*(*NICK *rises, opens his mouth to say something,
thinks better of it, exits)*
One more game.

MARTHA *(After* NICK *goes)*
I don't like what's going to happen.

GEORGE *(Surprisingly tender)*
Do you know what it is?

MARTHA *(Pathetic)*
No. But I don't like it.

GEORGE
Maybe you will, Martha.

MARTHA
No.

GEORGE
Oh, it's a real fun game, Martha.

MARTHA *(Pleading)*
No more games.

GEORGE *(Quietly triumphant)*
One more, Martha. One more game, and then beddie-
bye. Everybody pack up his tools and baggage and stuff

and go home. And you and me, well, we gonna climb
them well-worn stairs.

MARTHA *(Almost in tears)*

No, George; no.

GEORGE *(Soothing)*

Yes, baby.

MARTHA

No, George; please?

GEORGE

It'll all be done with before you know it.

MARTHA

No, George.

GEORGE

No climb stairs with Georgie?

MARTHA *(A sleepy child)*

No more games . . . please. It's games I don't want. No
more games.

GEORGE

Aw, sure you do, Martha . . . original game-girl and all,
course you do.

MARTHA

Ugly games . . . ugly. And now this new one?

GEORGE *(Stroking her hair)*

You'll love it, baby.

MARTHA

No, George.

GEORGE

You'll have a ball.

MARTHA
        (Tenderly; moves to touch him)
Please, George, no more games; I. . . .

GEORGE
        (Slapping her moving hand with vehemence)
Don't you touch me! You keep your paws clean for the
undergraduates!

MARTHA
        (A cry of alarm, but faint)

GEORGE
        (Grabbing her hair, pulling her head back)
Now, you listen to me, Martha; you have had quite an
evening . . . quite a night for yourself, and you can't just
cut it off whenever you've got enough blood in your
mouth. We are going on, and I'm going to have at you
and it's going to make your performance tonight look
like an Easter pageant. Now I want you to get yourself
a little alert. *(Slaps her lightly with his free hand)* I want
a little life in you, baby. *(Again)*

MARTHA *(Struggling)*
Stop it!

GEORGE
(Again) Pull yourself together! *(Again)* I want you on
your feet and slugging, sweetheart, because I'm going to
knock you around, and I want you up for it. *(Again; he
pulls away, releases her; she rises)*

MARTHA
All right, George. What do you want, George?

GEORGE

An equal battle, baby; that's all.

MARTHA

You'll get it!

GEORGE

I want you mad.

MARTHA

'M MAD!!

GEORGE

Get madder!

MARTHA

DON'T WORRY ABOUT IT!

GEORGE

Good for you, girl; now, we're going to play this one to the death.

MARTHA

Yours!

GEORGE

You'd be surprised. Now, here come the tots; you be ready for this.

MARTHA

(She paces, actually looks a bit like a fighter)
I'm ready for you.
(NICK and HONEY re-enter; NICK supporting HONEY, who still retains her brandy bottle and glass)

NICK *(Unhappily)*

Here we are.

HONEY *(Cheerfully)*

Hip, hop. Hip, hop.

NICK

You a bunny, Honey? *(She laughs greatly, sits)*

HONEY

I'm a bunny, Honey.

GEORGE *(To* HONEY*)*

Well, now; how's the bunny?

HONEY

Bunny funny! *(She laughs again)*

NICK *(Under his breath)*

Jesus.

GEORGE

Bunny funny? Good for bunny!

MARTHA

Come on, George!

GEORGE *(To* MARTHA*)*

Honey funny bunny! *(*HONEY *screams with laughter)*

NICK

Jesus God. . . .

GEORGE

(Slaps his hands together, once)

All right! Here we go! Last game! All sit. *(*NICK *sits)* S
down, Martha. This is a civilized game.

MARTHA

(Cocks her fist, doesn't swing)

(Sits) Just get on with it.

HONEY *(To GEORGE)*

I've decided I don't remember anything. *(To NICK)* Hello,
Dear.

GEORGE

Hunh? What?

MARTHA

It's almost dawn, for God's sake. . . .

HONEY *(Ibid)*

I don't remember anything, and you don't remember anything, either. Hello, Dear.

GEORGE

You what?

HONEY *(Ibid)*
(An edge creeping into her voice)
You heard me, nothing. Hello, Dear.

GEORGE
(To HONEY, referring to NICK)
You do know that's your husband, there, don't you?

HONEY *(With great dignity)*
Well, I certainly know *that*.

GEORGE *(Close to HONEY's ear)*
's just some things you can't remember . . . hunh?

HONEY
*(A great laugh to cover; then quietly, intensely
to GEORGE)*
on't remember; not *can't*. *(At NICK, cheerfully)* Hello,
ear.

GEORGE *(To* NICK)

Well, speak to your little wifelet, your little bunny, for God's sake.

NICK *(Softly, embarrassed)*

Hello, Honey.

GEORGE

Awww, that was nice. I think we've been having a . . . a real good evening . . . all things considered. . . . We've sat around, and got to know each other, and had fun and games . . . curl-up-on-the-floor, for example. . . .

HONEY

. . . the tiles. . . .

GEORGE

. . . the tiles. . . . Snap the Dragon.

HONEY

. . . peel the label. . . .

GEORGE

. . . peel the . . . what?

MARTHA

Label. Peel the label.

HONEY
(Apologetically, holding up her brandy bottle)
I peel labels.

GEORGE

We all peel labels, sweetie; and when you get through the skin, all three layers, through the muscle, slosh aside the organs *(An aside to* NICK) them which is still sloshable— *(Back to* HONEY) and get down to bone . . . you know what you do then?

HONEY *(Terribly interested)*

No!

GEORGE

When you get down to bone, you haven't got all the way, yet. There's something inside the bone . . . the marrow . . and that's what you gotta get at. *(A strange smile at* MARTHA*)*

HONEY

Oh! I see.

GEORGE

The marrow. But bones are pretty resilient, especially in the young. Now, take our son. . . .

HONEY *(Strangely)*

Who?

GEORGE

Our son. . . . Martha's and my little joy!

NICK
(Moving toward the bar)

Do you mind if I . . . ?

GEORGE

No, no; you go right ahead.

MARTHA

George. . . .

GEORGE *(Too kindly)*

Yes, Martha?

MARTHA

Just what are you doing?

GEORGE

Why love, I was talking about our son.

MARTHA

Don't.

GEORGE

Isn't Martha something? Here we are, on the eve of our boy's home-coming, the eve of his twenty-first birfday, the eve of his majority . . . and Martha says don't talk about him.

MARTHA

Just . . . don't.

GEORGE

But I want to, Martha! It's very important we talk about him. Now bunny and the . . . well, whichever he is . . here don't know much about junior, and I think they should.

MARTHA

Just . . . don't.

GEORGE
(Snapping his fingers at NICK*)*

You. Hey, you! You want to play Bringing Up Baby, don you!

NICK *(Hardly civil)*

Were you snapping at me?

GEORGE

That's right. *(Instructing him)* You want to hear abo our bouncey boy.

NICK *(Pause; then, shortly)*

Yeah; sure.

GEORGE *(To* HONEY*)*

And you, my dear? You want to hear about him, too, do you?

HONEY
(Pretending not to understand)

Whom?

GEORGE

Martha's and my son.

HONEY *(Nervously)*

Oh, you have a child?
(MARTHA *and* NICK *laugh uncomfortably*)

GEORGE

Oh, indeed; do we ever! Do you want to talk about him,
Martha, or shall I? Hunh?

MARTHA
(A smile that is a sneer)

Don't, George.

GEORGE

All rightie. Well, now; let's see. He's a nice kid, really, in
spite of his home life; I mean, most kids'd grow up
neurotic, what with Martha here carrying on the way she
does: sleeping 'till four in the P.M., climbing all over the
poor bastard, trying to break the bathroom door down to
wash him in the tub when he's sixteen, dragging strangers
into the house at all hours. . . .

MARTHA *(Rising)*

O.K. YOU!

GEORGE *(Mock concern)*

Martha!

MARTHA

That's enough!

GEORGE

Well, do you want to take over?

HONEY *(To* NICK*)*

Why would anybody want to wash somebody who's sixteen years old?

NICK
(Slamming his drink down)

Oh, for Christ's sake, Honey!

HONEY *(Stage whisper)*

Well, why?!

GEORGE

Because it's her baby-poo.

MARTHA

ALL RIGHT!!
(By rote; a kind of almost-tearful recitation)

Our son. You want our son? You'll have it.

GEORGE

You want a drink, Martha?

MARTHA *(Pathetically)*

Yes.

NICK *(To* MARTHA *kindly)*

We don't have to hear about it . . . if you don't want to

GEORGE

Who says so? You in a position to set the rules around here?

NICK *(Pause; tight-lipped)*

No.

GEORGE

Good boy; you'll go far. All right, Martha; your recitation, please.

MARTHA *(From far away)*

What, George?

GEORGE *(Prompting)*

"Our son. . . ."

MARTHA

All right. Our son. Our son was born in a September night, a night not unlike tonight, though tomorrow, and twenty . . . one . . . years ago.

GEORGE
(Beginning of quiet asides)

You see? I told you.

MARTHA

It was an easy birth. . . .

GEORGE

Oh, Martha; no. You labored . . . how you labored.

MARTHA

It was an easy birth . . . once it had been . . . accepted, relaxed into.

GEORGE

Ah . . . yes. Better.

MARTHA

It was an easy birth, once it had been accepted, and I was young.

GEORGE

And I was younger. . . . *(Laughs quietly to himself)*

MARTHA

And I was young, and he was a healthy child, a red, bawling child, with slippery firm limbs. . . .

GEORGE

. . . Martha thinks she saw him at delivery. . . .

MARTHA

. . . with slippery, firm limbs, and a full head of black, fine, fine hair which, oh, later, later, became blond as the sun, our son.

GEORGE

He was a healthy child.

MARTHA

And I had wanted a child . . . oh, I had wanted a child.

GEORGE *(Prodding her)*

A son? A daughter?

MARTHA

A child! *(Quieter)* A child. And I had my child.

GEORGE

Our child.

MARTHA *(With great sadness)*

Our child. And we raised him . . . *(Laughs, briefly, bitterly)* yes, we did; we raised him. . . .

GEORGE

With teddy bears and an antique bassinet from Austria . . . and *no nurse.*

MARTHA

. . . with teddy bears and transparent floating goldfish, and a pale blue bed with cane at the headboard when he was older, cane which he wore through . . . finally . . . with his little hands . . . in his . . . sleep. . . .

GEORGE

. . . nightmares. . . .

MARTHA

. . . *sleep.* . . . He was a restless child. . . .

GEORGE

. . . *(Soft chuckle, head-shaking of disbelief)* . . . Oh Lord . . .

MARTHA

. . . sleep . . . and a croup tent . . . a pale green croup tent, and the shining kettle hissing in the one light of the room that time he was sick . . . those four days . . . and animal crackers, and the bow and arrow he kept under his bed. . . .

GEORGE

. . . the arrows with rubber cups at their tip. . . .

MARTHA

. . . at their tip, which he kept beneath his bed. . . .

GEORGE

Why? Why, Martha?

MARTHA

. . . for fear . . . for fear of. . . .

GEORGE

For fear. Just that: for fear.

MARTHA
(Vaguely waving him off; going on)

... and ... and sandwiches on Sunday night, and Saturdays ... *(Pleased recollection)* ... and Saturdays the banana boat, the whole peeled banana, scooped out on top, with green grapes for the crew, a double line of green grapes, and along the sides, stuck to the boat with toothpicks, orange slices.... SHIELDS.

GEORGE

And for the oar?

MARTHA *(Uncertainly)*

A ... carrot?

GEORGE

Or a swizzle stick, whatever was easier.

MARTHA

No. A carrot. And his eyes were green ... green with ... if you peered so deep into them ... so deep ... bronze ... bronze parentheses around the irises ... such green eyes!

GEORGE

... blue, green, brown. ...

MARTHA

... and he loved the sun! ... He was tan before and after everyone ... and in the sun his hair ... became ... fleece.

GEORGE *(Echoing her)*

... fleece. ...

MARTHA

... beautiful, beautiful boy.

GEORGE

Absolve, Domine, animas omnium fidelium defunctorum ab omni vinculo delictorum.

MARTHA

. . . and school . . . and summer camp . . . and sledding . . . and swimming. . . .

GEORGE

Et gratia tua illis succurrente, mereantur evadere judicium ultionis.

MARTHA *(Laughing, to herself)*

. . . and how he broke his arm . . . how funny it was . . . oh, no, it hurt him! . . . but, oh, it was funny . . . in a field, his very first cow, the first he'd ever seen . . . and he went into the field, to the cow, where the cow was grazing, head down, busy . . . and he moo'd at it! *(Laughs, ibid)* He moo'd at it . . . and the beast, oh, surprised, swung its head up and moo'd at him, all three years of him, and he ran, startled, and he stumbled . . . fell . . . and broke his poor arm. *(Laughs, ibid)* Poor lamb.

GEORGE

Et lucis aeternae beatitudine perfrui.

MARTHA

George cried! Helpless . . . George . . . cried. I carried the poor lamb. George snuffling beside me, I carried the child, having fashioned a sling . . . and across the great fields.

GEORGE

In Paradisum deducant te Angeli.

MARTHA

And as he grew . . . and as he grew . . . oh! so wise! . . . he walked evenly between us . . . *(She spreads her hands)* . . . a hand out to each of us for what we could offer by way of support, affection, teaching, even love . . . and these hands, still, to hold us off a bit, for mutual protection, to protect us all from George's . . . weakness . . . and my . . . necessary greater strength . . . to protect himself . . . and *us*.

GEORGE

In memoria aeterna erit justus: ab auditione mala non timebit.

MARTHA

So wise; so wise.

NICK (*To* GEORGE)

What is this? What are you doing?

GEORGE

Shhhhh.

HONEY

Shhhhh.

NICK (*Shrugging*)

O.K.

MARTHA

So beautiful; so wise.

GEORGE (*Laughs quietly*)

All truth being relative.

MARTHA

It was true! Beautiful; wise; perfect.

GEORGE

There's a real mother talking.

HONEY
(*Suddenly; almost tearfully*)

I want a child.

NICK

Honey. . . .

HONEY *(More forcefully)*

I want a child!

GEORGE

On principle?

HONEY *(in tears)*

I want a child. I want a baby.

MARTHA

(Waiting out the interruption, not really paying it any mind)

Of course, this state, this perfection . . . couldn't last. Not with George . . . not with George around.

GEORGE *(To the others)*

There; you see? I knew she'd shift.

HONEY

Be still!

GEORGE *(Mock awe)*

Sorry . . . mother.

NICK

Can't you be still?

GEORGE *(Making a sign at* NICK*)*

Dominus vobiscum.

MARTHA

Not with George around. A drowning man takes down those nearest. George tried, but, oh, God, how I fought him. God, how I fought him.

GEORGE *(A satisfied laugh)*

hhhhhh.

MARTHA

esser states can't stand those above them. Weakness.

imperfection cries out against strength, goodness and
innocence. And George tried.

GEORGE
How did I try, Martha? How did I try?

MARTHA
How did you . . . what? . . . No! No . . . he grew . . .
our son grew . . . up; he is grown up; he is away at school,
college. He is fine, everything is fine.

GEORGE *(Mocking)*
Oh, come on, Martha!

MARTHA
No. That's all.

GEORGE
Just a minute! You can't cut a story off like that, sweet
heart. You started to say something . . . now you say it

MARTHA
No!

GEORGE
Well, I will.

MARTHA
No!

GEORGE
You see, Martha, here, stops just when the going ge
good . . . just when things start getting a little rough. Nov
Martha, here, is a misunderstood little girl; she really i
Not only does she have a husband who is a bog . . .
younger-than-she-is bog albeit . . . not only does she hav
a husband who is a bog, she has as well a tiny proble
with spiritous liquors—like she can't get enough. . . .

MARTHA *(Without energy)*

No more, George.

GEORGE

. . . and on top of all that, poor weighed-down girl, PLUS a father who really doesn't give a damn whether she lives or dies, who couldn't care less *what* happens to his only daughter . . . on top of all that she has a *son*. She has a son who fought her every inch of the way, who didn't want to be turned into a weapon against his father, who didn't want to be used as a goddamn club whenever Martha didn't get things like she wanted them!

MARTHA *(Rising to it)*

Lies! Lies!!

GEORGE

Lies? All right. A son who would *not* disown his father, who came to him for advice, for information, for love that wasn't mixed with sickness—and you know what I mean, Martha!—who could not tolerate the slashing, braying residue that called itself his MOTHER. MOTHER? HAH!!

MARTHA *(Cold)*

All right, you. A son who was so ashamed of his father he asked me once if it—possibly—wasn't true, as he had heard, from some cruel boys, maybe, that he was not our child; who could not tolerate the shabby failure his father had become. . . .

GEORGE

Lies!

MARTHA

Lies? Who would not bring his girl friends to the house. . . .

GEORGE

... in shame of his mother. ...

MARTHA

... of his father! Who writes letters only to me!

GEORGE

Oh, so you think! To me! At my office!

MARTHA

Liar!

GEORGE

I have a stack of them!

MARTHA

YOU HAVE NO LETTERS!

GEORGE

And you have?

MARTHA

He has no letters. A son ... a son who spends his summers
away ... away from his family ... ON ANY PRETEXT ..
because he can't stand the shadow of a man flickering
around the edges of a house. ...

GEORGE

... who spends his summers away ... and he does! ..
who spends his summers away because there isn't room
for him in a house full of empty bottles, lies, strange men
and a harridan who. ...

MARTHA

Liar!!

GEORGE

Liar?

MARTHA

... A son who I have raised as best I can against ..

vicious odds, against the corruption of weakness and petty revenges. . . .

GEORGE

. . . A son who is, deep in his gut, sorry to have been born. . . .

(BOTH TOGETHER)

MARTHA	GEORGE
I have tried, oh God I have tried; the one thing . . . the one thing I've tried to carry pure and unscathed through the sewer of this marriage; through the sick nights, and the pathetic, stupid days, through the derision and the laughter . . . *God*, the laughter, through one failure after another, one failure compounding another failure, each attempt more sickening, more numbing than the one before; the one thing, the one *person* I have tried to protect, to raise above the mire of this vile, crushing marriage; the one light in all this hopeless . . . darkness . . . our SON.	Libera me, Domine, de morte aeterna, in die illa tremenda: Quando caeli movendi sunt et terra: Dum veneris judicare saeculum per ignem. Tremens factus sum ego, et timeo, dum discussio venerit, atque ventura ira. Quando caeli movendi sunt et terra. Dies illa, dies irae, calamitatis et miseriae; dies magna et amara valde. Dum veneris judicare saeculum per ignem. Requiem aeternam dona eis, Domine: et lux perpetua luceat eis. Libera me Domine de morte aeterna in die illa tremenda: quando caeli movendi sunt et terra; Dum veneris judicare saeculum per ignem.

(End together)

HONEY *(Her hands to her ears)*

STOP IT!! STOP IT!!

GEORGE *(With a hand sign)*

Kyrie, eleison. Christe, eleison. Kyrie, eleison.

HONEY

JUST STOP IT!!

GEORGE

Why, baby? Don't you like it?

HONEY *(Quite hysterical)*

You . . . can't . . . do . . . this!

GEORGE *(Triumphant)*

Who says!

HONEY

I! Say!

GEORGE

Tell us why, baby.

HONEY

No!

NICK

Is this game over?

HONEY

Yes! Yes, it is.

GEORGE

Ho-ho! Not by a long shot. *(To* MARTHA*)* We got a little
surprise for you, baby. It's about sunny-Jim.

MARTHA

No more, George.

GEORGE

YES!

NICK

Leave her be!

GEORGE

I'M RUNNING THIS SHOW! *(To* MARTHA*)* Sweetheart, I'm afraid I've got some bad news for you . . . for us, of course. Some rather sad news.

(HONEY *begins weeping, head in hands)*

MARTHA *(Afraid, suspicious)*

What is this?

GEORGE *(Oh, so patiently)*

Well, Martha, while you were out of the room, while the . . . two of you were out of the room . . . I mean, I don't know where, hell, you both must have been somewhere *(Little laugh)*. . . . While you were out of the room, for a while . . . well, Missey and I were sittin' here havin' a little talk, you know: a chaw and a talk . . . and the door-bell rang. . . .

HONEY *(Head still in hands)*

Chimed.

GEORGE

Chimed . . . and . . . well, it's hard to tell you, Martha. . . .

MARTHA
(A strange throaty voice)

Tell me.

HONEY

Please . . . don't.

MARTHA

Tell me.

GEORGE

. . . and . . . what it was . . . it was good old Western

Union, some little boy about seventy.

MARTHA *(Involved)*

Crazy Billy?

GEORGE

Yes, Martha, that's right . . . crazy Billy . . . and he had a
telegram, and it was for us, and I have to tell you about
it.

MARTHA
(As if from a distance)

Why didn't they phone it? Why did they bring it; why
didn't they telephone it?

GEORGE

Some telegrams you have to deliver, Martha; some telegrams you can't phone.

MARTHA *(Rising)*

What do you mean?

GEORGE

Martha. . . . I can hardly bring myself to say it. . . .

HONEY

Don't.

GEORGE *(To* HONEY*)*

Do you want to do it?

HONEY
(Defending herself against an attack of bees)

No no no no no.

GEORGE *(Sighing heavily)*

All right. Well, Martha . . . I'm afraid our boy isn't coming
home for his birthday.

MARTHA

Of course he is.

GEORGE

No, Martha.

MARTHA

Of course he is. I say he is!

GEORGE

He . . . can't.

MARTHA

He is! I say so!

GEORGE

Martha . . . *(Long pause)* . . . our son is . . . dead.
(Silence)
He was . . . killed . . . late in the afternoon. . . .
(Silence)
(A tiny chuckle) on a country road, with his learner's permit in his pocket, he swerved, to avoid a porcupine, and drove straight into a. . . .

MARTHA *(Rigid fury)*

YOU . . . CAN'T . . . DO . . . THAT!

GEORGE

. . . large tree.

MARTHA

YOU CANNOT DO THAT!

NICK *(Softly)*

Oh my God. (HONEY *is weeping louder*)

GEORGE
(Quietly, dispassionately)

I thought you should know.

NICK

Oh my God; no.

MARTHA
(*Quivering with rage and loss*)
NO! NO! YOU CANNOT DO THAT! YOU CAN'T DECIDE THAT FOR
YOURSELF! I WILL NOT LET YOU DO THAT!

GEORGE

We'll have to leave around noon, I suppose. . . .

MARTHA

I WILL NOT LET YOU DECIDE THESE THINGS!

GEORGE

. . . because there are matters of identification, naturally,
and arrangements to be made. . . .

MARTHA
(*Leaping at* GEORGE, *but ineffectual*)
YOU CAN'T DO THIS!
(NICK *rises, grabs hold of* MARTHA, *pins her arms be-
hind her back*)
I WON'T LET YOU DO THIS, GET YOUR HANDS OFF ME!

GEORGE
(*As* NICK *holds on; right in* MARTHA'S *face*)
You don't seem to understand, Martha; I haven't done
anything. Now, pull yourself together. Our son is DEAD!
Can you get that into your head?

MARTHA

YOU CAN'T DECIDE THESE THINGS.

NICK

Lady, please.

MARTHA

LET ME GO!

GEORGE

Now listen, Martha; listen carefully. We got a telegram; there was a car accident, and he's dead. POUF! Just like that! Now, how do you like it?

MARTHA
(A howl which weakens into a moan)
NOOOOOOooooooo.

GEORGE *(To* NICK)
Let her go. (MARTHA *slumps to the floor in a sitting position)* She'll be all right now.

MARTHA *(Pathetic)*
No; no, he is *not* dead; he is not *dead*.

GEORGE
He is dead. Kyrie, eleison. Christe, eleison. Kyrie, eleison.

MARTHA
You can*not*. You may not decide these things.

NICK
(Leaning over her; tenderly)
He hasn't decided anything, lady. It's not his doing. He doesn't have the power. . . .

GEORGE
That's right, Martha; I'm not a God. I don't have the power over life and death, do I?

MARTHA
YOU CAN'T KILL HIM! YOU CAN'T HAVE HIM DIE!

HONEY
Lady . . . please. . . .

MARTHA

YOU CAN'T!

GEORGE

There was a telegram, Martha.

MARTHA *(Up; facing him)*

Show it to me! Show me the telegram!

GEORGE
(Long pause; then, with a straight face)

I ate it.

MARTHA
*(A pause; then with the greatest disbelief possible,
tinged with hysteria)*

What did you just say to me?

GEORGE
(Barely able to stop exploding with laughter)

I . . . ate . . . it.
*(MARTHA stares at him for a long moment, then
spits in his face)*

GEORGE *(With a smile)*

Good for you, Martha.

NICK *(To GEORGE)*

Do you think that's the way to treat her at a time like
this? Making an ugly goddamn joke like that? Hunh?

GEORGE
(Snapping his fingers at HONEY)

Did I eat the telegram or did I not?

HONEY *(Terrified)*

Yes; yes, you ate it. I watched . . . I watched you . . . you

. . . you ate it all down.

GEORGE *(Prompting)*

. . . like a good boy.

HONEY

. . . like a . . . g-g-g-good . . . boy. Yes.

MARTHA *(To GEORGE, coldly)*

You're not going to get away with this.

GEORGE *(With disgust)*

YOU KNOW THE RULES, MARTHA! FOR CHRIST'S SAKE, YOU KNOW THE RULES!

MARTHA

NO!

NICK

(With the beginnings of a knowledge he cannot face)
What are you two talking about?

GEORGE

I can kill him, Martha, if I want to.

MARTHA

HE IS OUR CHILD!

GEORGE

Oh yes, and you bore him, and it was a good delivery. . . .

MARTHA

HE IS OUR CHILD!

GEORGE

AND I HAVE KILLED HIM!

MARTHA

NO!

GEORGE

YES!

(Long silence)

NICK *(Very quietly)*

I think I understand this.

GEORGE *(Ibid)*

Do you?

NICK *(Ibid)*

Jesus Christ, I think I understand this.

GEORGE *(Ibid)*

Good for you, buster.

NICK *(Violently)*

JESUS CHRIST I THINK I UNDERSTAND THIS!

MARTHA

(Great sadness and loss)

You have no right . . . you have no right at all. . . .

GEORGE *(Tenderly)*

I have the right, Martha. We never spoke of it; that's all.
I could kill him any time I wanted to.

MARTHA

But why? Why?

GEORGE

You broke our rule, baby. You mentioned him . . . you
mentioned him to someone else.

MARTHA *(Tearfully)*

I did *not*. I never did.

GEORGE

Yes, you did.

MARTHA

Who? who?

HONEY *(Crying)*

To me. You mentioned him to me.

MARTHA *(Crying)*

I FORGET! Sometimes . . . sometimes when it's night, when it's late, and . . . and everybody else is . . . talking . . . I forget and I . . . want to mention him . . . but I . . . HOLD ON . . . I hold on . . . but I've wanted to . . . so often . . . oh, George, you've *pushed* it . . . there was no need . . . there was no need for *this*. I *men*tioned him . . . all right . . . but you didn't have to push it over the EDGE. You didn't have to . . . kill him.

GEORGE

Requiescat in pace.

HONEY

Amen.

MARTHA

You didn't have to have him die, George.

GEORGE

Requiem aeternam dona eis, Domine.

HONEY

Et lux perpetua luceat eis.

MARTHA

That wasn't . . . needed.

(*A long silence*)

GEORGE *(Softly)*

It will be dawn soon. I think the party's over.

NICK (*To* GEORGE; *quietly*)

You couldn't have . . . any?

GEORGE

We couldn't.

MARTHA
(*A hint of communion in this*)

We couldn't.

GEORGE (*To* NICK *and* HONEY)

Home to bed, children; it's way past your bedtime.

NICK (*His hand out to* HONEY)

Honey?

HONEY
(*Rising, moving to him*)

Yes.

GEORGE
(MARTHA *is sitting on the floor by a chair now*)

You two go now.

NICK

Yes.

HONEY

Yes.

NICK

I'd like to. . . .

GEORGE

Good night.

NICK (*Pause*)

Good night.

(NICK *and* HONEY *exit;* GEORGE *closes the door after them; looks around the room; sighs, picks up a glass or two, takes it to the bar)*
(This whole last section very softly, very slowly)

GEORGE

Do you want anything, Martha?

MARTHA *(Still looking away)*

No . . . nothing.

GEORGE

All right. *(Pause)* Time for bed.

MARTHA

Yes.

GEORGE

re you tired?

MARTHA

Yes.

GEORGE

am.

MARTHA

es.

GEORGE

unday tomorrow; all day.

MARTHA

es.

(A long silence between them)
id you . . . did you . . . have to?

GEORGE *(Pause)*

Yes.

MARTHA

It was . . . ? You had to?

GEORGE *(Pause)*

Yes.

MARTHA

I don't know.

GEORGE

It was . . . time.

MARTHA

Was it?

GEORGE

Yes.

MARTHA *(Pause)*

I'm cold.

GEORGE

It's late.

MARTHA

Yes.

GEORGE *(Long silence)*

It will be better.

MARTHA *(Long silence)*

I don't . . . know.

GEORGE

It will be . . . maybe.

MARTHA

I'm . . . not . . . sure.

GEORGE

No.

MARTHA

Just . . . us?

GEORGE

Yes.

MARTHA

I don't suppose, maybe, we could. . . .

GEORGE

No, Martha.

MARTHA

Yes. No.

GEORGE

Are you all right?

MARTHA

Yes. No.

GEORGE

(Puts his hand gently on her shoulder; she puts her head back and he sings to her, very softly)
Who's afraid of Virginia Woolf,
          Virginia Woolf,
          Virginia Woolf,

MARTHA

I . . . am . . . George. . . .

GEORGE
Who's afraid of Virginia Woolf. . . .

MARTHA
I . . . am . . . George. . . . I . . . am. . . .
                    (GEORGE *nods, slowly*)
                    (*Silence; tableau*)

CURTAIN

TINY
ALICE

77097/95¢

by

EDWARD
ALBEE

"ONE OF THE MOST SIGNIFICANT PLAYS
IN THE HISTORY OF THE THEATRE"
—NEWSWEEK

Author of

WHO'S AFRAID OF VIRGINIA WOOLF?

77100/95¢

A DELICATE BALANCE...95072/95¢

If your bookseller does not have these titles, you
may order them by sending retail price, plus 15¢
for mailing and handling to: MAIL SERVICE
DEPARTMENT, Pocket Books, a division of Simon
& Schuster, Inc., 1 W. 39th St., New York, N.Y.
10018. Not responsible for orders containing cash.
Please send check or money order.

Published by POCKET BOOKS

A 10/9

HAROLD ROBBINS
THE ADVENTURERS

12501/$1.25

Other titles by Harold Robbins:

If your bookseller does not have these titles, you may order them by sending retail price, plus 15¢ for mailing and handling to: MAIL SERVICE DEPARTMENT, POCKET BOOKS, A Division of Simon & Schuster, Inc., 1 West 39th St., New York, N.Y. 10018. Not responsible for orders containing cash. Please send check or money order.

PUBLISHED BY
POCKET BOOKS

A 7/9

Winner of the 1965-66 Season
New York
Drama Critics' Circle
and Tony Awards
now a UNITED ARTISTS
picture.

75178/75c

THE PERSECUTION
AND ASSASSINATION
OF JEAN PAUL MARAT
AS PERFORMED BY THE INMATES
OF THE ASYLUM OF CHARENTON
UNDER THE DIRECTION
OF THE MARQUIS DE SADE
by PETER WEISS

Another engrossing chapter in the
continuing story of the town
made famous by the best-selling
novels of GRACE METALIOUS

Secrets of Peyton Place

by ROGER FULLER

75285/75¢

Other titles:

If your bookseller does not have these titles, you may
order them by sending retail price, plus 15¢ for mailing and handling to: MAIL SERVICE DEPARTMENT,
POCKET BOOKS, A Division of Simon & Schuster,
Inc., 1 West 39th St., New York, N. Y. 10018. Not
responsible for orders containing cash. Please send
check or money order.

PUBLISHED BY
POCKET BOOKS
A 9/9